TALES OF
THE PREHISTORIC WORLD

NEON SQUID

CONTENTS

4 Welcome to the prehistoric world!

6 A journey through time

8 The big five extinctions

10 The beginning

12 Prehistoric goo and the Mars rover

14 The kids of Charnwood Forest

16 Life begins to get complicated

18 An explosion of life

20 The amazing discoveries at Burgess Shale

22 The king of the trilobites

24 Secrets of the fossils

26 The age of armored fish

28 The walking fish

30 Meet the giant bugs

32 The mystery of the buzzsaw shark

34 The family in the burrow

36 The age of reptiles

38 The supercontinent of Pangaea

40 The Triassic footprints

42 What exactly is a dinosaur?

44 The rancher's delight

46 Rulers of the Triassic

48 The baby-eaters

50 The first giants

52 Weird life of the Triassic

54 The 3D pterosaur

56 The frozen reptile

58 Mary Anning: fossil hunter

60 The megaraft

62 The missing bones

64 Dino death trap

66 Flight, fuzz, and feathers

68 The sad story of Big Al

70 The Bone Wars

72 A tale in two parts

74 The final supper

76 The secrets of the mine

78 The spiny sauropod

80 The beasts of prehistoric China

82 The colorful Psittacosaurus

84 The wonders of Las Hoyas

86 The block of raptors

88 Shape-shifting dinosaurs

90 The seafaring ankylosaur

92 The giant of giants

94 The gemstone dinosaurs

96 Creatures of the shallow sea

98 Searching for Spinosaurus

102 Fight to the death

104 Egg Mountain

106 Musical monsters

108 Meet the frilly dinosaurs

110 Triceratops vs. Torosaurus

112 Mystery of the stolen fossils

114 Clash of the boneheads

116 The giant pterosaurs

118 King of the tyrant lizards

120 T. rex grows up

122 The crater of doom

124 The recent past

126 The age of mammals

128 The monster snake

130 The evil winds

132 The creatures of Turtle Cove

134 The giant rhino

136 Meet the mega shark

138 Treasures from the dump

140 The world turns to ash

142 The whale graveyard

144 The people in the trees

146 The dawn of humans

148 The pit of despair

150 Giants of the Ice Age

152 The last mammoths

154 Glossary

156 Index

160 Acknowledgments

WELCOME TO THE PREHISTORIC WORLD!

I LOVE ancient life and the fossils it leaves behind. From prehistoric goo to dinosaurs to our most recent extinct ancestors, I find everything fascinating. My passion for fossils started when I was maybe around your age. The place I grew up in was at the bottom of an ocean 305 million years ago! I would find whole shells in limestone that were filled with crystals. On the playground, I spent my school breaks searching for pieces of crinoids, or sea lilies. Being the first human to hold a fossil is a feeling that has never left me.

Luckily I had the privilege to chase my dream of becoming a paleontologist. I study the history of life using fossils. Being a paleontologist is similar to being a detective—we use fossils as clues to figure out what life was like in the remote past. Now, fossils represent life that is really, really dead. I'll never actually get to observe any of it. But learning all that we can about

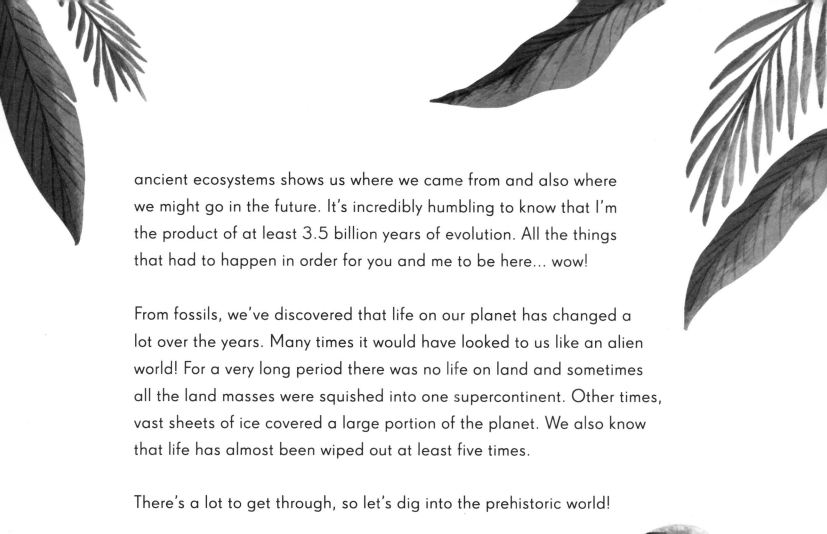

ancient ecosystems shows us where we came from and also where we might go in the future. It's incredibly humbling to know that I'm the product of at least 3.5 billion years of evolution. All the things that had to happen in order for you and me to be here... wow!

From fossils, we've discovered that life on our planet has changed a lot over the years. Many times it would have looked to us like an alien world! For a very long period there was no life on land and sometimes all the land masses were squished into one supercontinent. Other times, vast sheets of ice covered a large portion of the planet. We also know that life has almost been wiped out at least five times.

There's a lot to get through, so let's dig into the prehistoric world!

Kallie Moore

A JOURNEY THROUGH TIME

Earth's life has changed a lot since it emerged around 3.5 billion years ago. Those changes have been recorded in rocks! If the conditions are just right when a creature dies, it can turn into a fossil—preserved in the rock. Younger rocks are deposited on top of older rocks, and each layer represents a chunk of time. To organize these layers, scientists created something called the Geological Time Scale.

Champsosaurus (Paleocene)

Uintatherium (Eocene)

Stegosaurus (Jurassic)

Tullimonstrum (Carboniferous)

Dunkleosteus (Devonian)

Platystrophia (Ordovician)

Elrathia (Cambrian)

Cenozoic

Life is currently in the Age of Mammals. This is where the human family tree starts. Over the past 66 million years, shrewlike insect-eaters evolved into two-legged tool-makers (that's you) and spread around the globe.

Mesozoic

Dinosaurs ruled the Earth during the Age of Reptiles. Their reign ended when a giant space rock crashed into Earth.

Paleozoic

There was an explosion of life at the beginning of the Paleozoic. Life moved from the water to the land. The period ended with the largest mass extinction ever.

Precambrian

Simple life-forms emerged in the Precambrian, around a billion years after Earth formed.

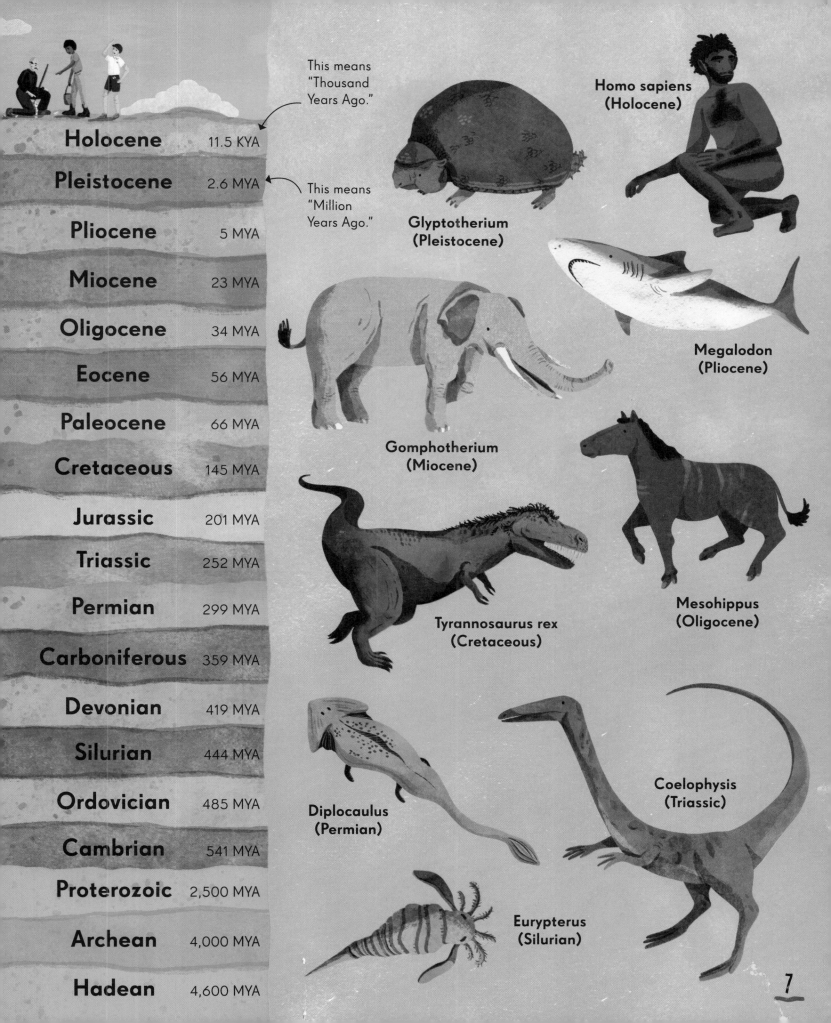

Holocene	11.5 KYA
Pleistocene	2.6 MYA
Pliocene	5 MYA
Miocene	23 MYA
Oligocene	34 MYA
Eocene	56 MYA
Paleocene	66 MYA
Cretaceous	145 MYA
Jurassic	201 MYA
Triassic	252 MYA
Permian	299 MYA
Carboniferous	359 MYA
Devonian	419 MYA
Silurian	444 MYA
Ordovician	485 MYA
Cambrian	541 MYA
Proterozoic	2,500 MYA
Archean	4,000 MYA
Hadean	4,600 MYA

This means "Thousand Years Ago."

This means "Million Years Ago."

Glyptotherium
(Pleistocene)

Homo sapiens
(Holocene)

Megalodon
(Pliocene)

Gomphotherium
(Miocene)

Tyrannosaurus rex
(Cretaceous)

Mesohippus
(Oligocene)

Diplocaulus
(Permian)

Coelophysis
(Triassic)

Eurypterus
(Silurian)

7

THE BIG FIVE
EXTINCTIONS

More than 95% of all species that have ever lived are now extinct. When more than 50% of life disappears in less than a million years, it is called a mass extinction. Luckily, these events are rare! They have only happened five times during the history of our planet. And they all have one thing in common: climate change. At various points Earth has rapidly got really hot or really cold, with devastating consequences.

444 MYA

Trilobites   **Graptolites**

Ordovician

Life was mainly in the oceans when 85% of species went extinct. Animals like trilobites and graptolites survived but took a hit. This extinction occurred in two parts. There was major cooling followed by a rapid warming. Possible causes include the effects of newly evolved plants and volcanic eruptions.

359 MYA

Placoderms

Devonian

During the Devonian, the first forests spread across the land. This caused the climate to cool. Ice sheets formed, causing sea levels to drop. This devastated marine communities. By the end of the Devonian, 75% of life went extinct, including armored fish called placoderms.

Permian

This extinction is known as the "Great Dying" because over 95% of life on Earth went extinct! In Siberia, the ground cracked open and lava poured out. These eruptions wreaked havoc and caused extreme global warming.

252 MYA

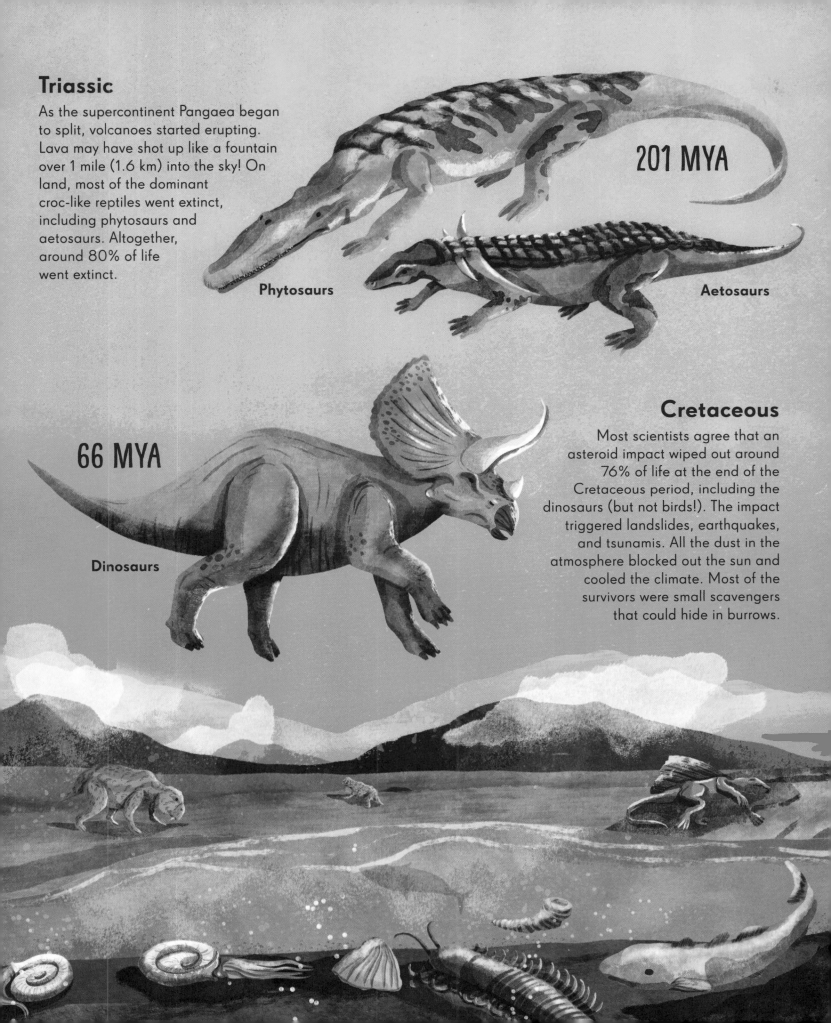

Triassic

As the supercontinent Pangaea began to split, volcanoes started erupting. Lava may have shot up like a fountain over 1 mile (1.6 km) into the sky! On land, most of the dominant croc-like reptiles went extinct, including phytosaurs and aetosaurs. Altogether, around 80% of life went extinct.

201 MYA

Phytosaurs

Aetosaurs

66 MYA

Dinosaurs

Cretaceous

Most scientists agree that an asteroid impact wiped out around 76% of life at the end of the Cretaceous period, including the dinosaurs (but not birds!). The impact triggered landslides, earthquakes, and tsunamis. All the dust in the atmosphere blocked out the sun and cooled the climate. Most of the survivors were small scavengers that could hide in burrows.

CHAPTER ONE
THE BEGINNING

Welcome to the Precambrian. While this is the shortest chapter in the book, this period represents almost 90% of our planet's history. It starts with the formation of Earth, roughly 4.6 billion years ago, and ends 541 million years ago. We'll start 3.5 billion years ago with the oldest confirmed life: the humble stromatolite. Then we'll fast-forward through almost two billion years to check out the earliest complex life. Most of it was squishy!

PREHISTORIC GOO AND THE MARS ROVER

Our first story starts roughly 3.5 billion years ago, in an area that would later become part of Australia. Here, in shallow marine environments, lived a type of bacteria that got its energy from sunlight. The bacteria formed mounds by trapping sediment in their goo, building up layers as they grew toward the light. These structures are called **stromatolites**. Incredibly, some are still alive today!

Fossil stromatolites are the oldest evidence of life on Earth—and none are more ancient than those from Strelley Pool in Western Australia. Scientists have been studying them for more than 40 years and have found six different types. Compared to a T. rex skeleton they don't look like much, just lumps and bumps, but they show that life was already active on our planet billions of years ago.

Recently, space scientists have become interested in the Strelley Pool stromatolites. This is because at the time these stromatolites were first alive, over three billion years ago, **Mars** is thought to have had water—even oceans! And since stromatolites are the most easily identifiable evidence of early life, researchers used the ones on Earth to test experiments that could be performed on Mars. Then it was time for the real thing...

In 2020, the rover Perseverance blasted off from Earth, headed toward the Red Planet. Its main job was to **look for signs of life** and collect samples of rock. On February 18, 2021, the rover landed in Jezero Crater, where the remains of ancient rivers and a lake had been spotted. It's possible that bacterial life may have lived in this lake, so Perseverance started investigating. On September 6, 2021, the rover collected its first Martian rock sample using a special drill. The rock will be stored in an airtight container until future missions can bring it back to Earth. Who knows what it might reveal?

THE KIDS OF CHARNWOOD FOREST

In England in the 1840s, odd ringlike structures were found in the rocks of Charnwood Forest by some quarrymen. Locals came to know the quarry as the "ring pit," but they didn't know what the rings were. A few years later an amateur geologist (someone who studies rocks) named Sir Andrew Crombie Ramsay suggested they might be **fossils**, but professional scientists told him that it was impossible! They explained that the rocks were too old—from the Precambrian— and that no fossilized life-forms had ever been found from that time.

Almost 100 years later a teenager named Tina Negus was out picking berries in the Charnwood Forest quarry. At the base of a cliff she spotted some **weird leaflike patterns**. She showed her teacher, who also told her they couldn't possibly be fossils. Tina wasn't discouraged though. She returned to the site to make a rubbing of the rock with a piece of paper and a pencil. After visiting museums and looking in books, she was stumped. Her fossil didn't match anything she could find.

The following year, in 1957, three boys—Roger Mason, Richard Blachford, and Richard Allen—were climbing in the same old quarry. They found the impressions and Roger, knowing a bit about geology, also thought they could be fossils. He went to a local university and spoke with Professor Trevor Ford, a geologist, who was skeptical. Are you seeing a trend here?

So Roger went ahead and did a rubbing of his own. He brought it back to the professor, who immediately drove to Charnwood Forest. Professor Ford was shocked—they *were* fossils! Roger, Tina, and Sir Andrew had been right all along.

Professor Ford used chisels, hammers, and crowbars to lever out a giant block containing the specimens. He announced the fossils to the world in 1958, naming the leaflike impressions **Charnia**. They are the first recognized Precambrian fossils and are thought to be between 569 and 556 million years old. The ringlike fossils were named Charniodiscus and were thought to be holdfasts, structures that attached the animals to the seafloor. It was an incredible discovery—and all thanks to the kids of Charnwood Forest!

LIFE BEGINS TO GET
COMPLICATED

The earliest known complex life on Earth appeared around 600 million years ago, during the Precambrian. These early life-forms are called the Ediacaran Biota, and they lived until about 542 million years ago. Scientists don't know if they are directly related to later animals or if they represent a separate branch of the family tree.

Tribrachidium lived in shallow water. It was a soft-bodied creature unlike anything alive today.

Cloudina had one of the first hard shells and was possibly a worm. It looked like stacked tubes.

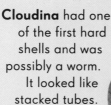

Kimberella was a snail-like creature that scraped food off the seafloor.

Fractofusus may have reproduced by growing its own clones!

A different Earth

Using rocks and fossils, scientists can track the ancient position of the oceans and continents as they moved over time. The Earth didn't always look like it does today! During the late Precambrian the land was just exposed rock, with all life living in the oceans. Ediacaran Biota fossils have been found all over the world, from South Australia to Canada.

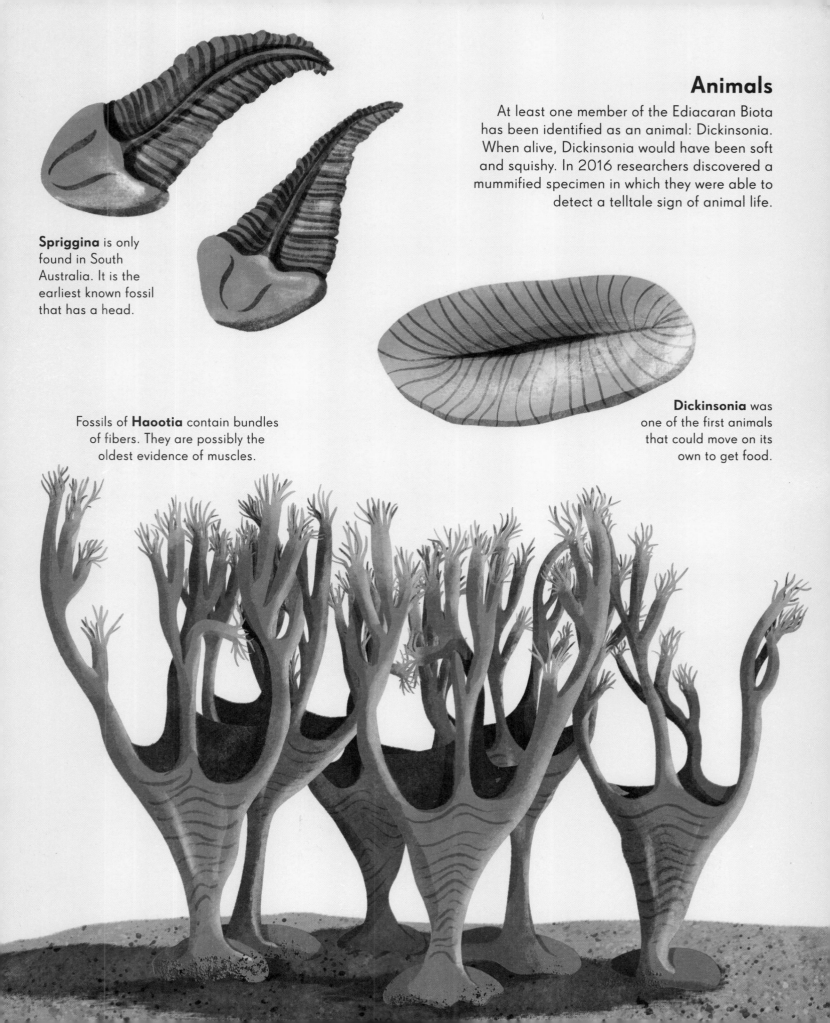

Animals

At least one member of the Ediacaran Biota has been identified as an animal: Dickinsonia. When alive, Dickinsonia would have been soft and squishy. In 2016 researchers discovered a mummified specimen in which they were able to detect a telltale sign of animal life.

Spriggina is only found in South Australia. It is the earliest known fossil that has a head.

Fossils of **Haootia** contain bundles of fibers. They are possibly the oldest evidence of muscles.

Dickinsonia was one of the first animals that could move on its own to get food.

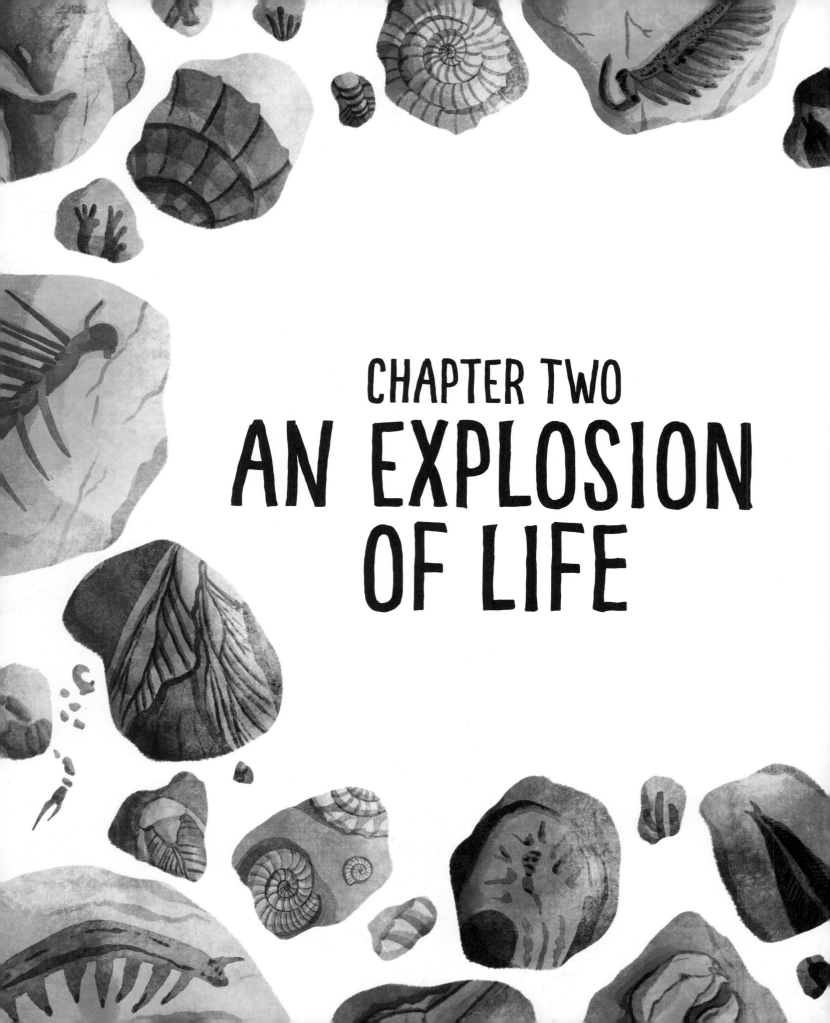

CHAPTER TWO
AN EXPLOSION OF LIFE

The Paleozoic lasted from 541 to 252 million years ago. All of the major groups of animals appeared in the Cambrian, around 500 million years ago. Later we saw the arrival of king-sized trilobites, armored fish, and giant bugs! A supercontinent called Pangaea formed and stretched from pole to pole. And then, just when it was really getting going, almost all life was annihilated during the largest mass extinction in our planet's history.

Vauxia was a simple branching sponge that belongs to the same group as today's harvested bath sponges. And like modern sponges it lived by filtering tiny food particles from the water.

THE AMAZING DISCOVERIES AT
BURGESS SHALE

During the construction of the Canadian Pacific Railway in 1909, Charles Walcott discovered the now famous Burgess Shale fossils. The creatures found in the Burgess Shale date back to the Cambrian, 510–505 million years ago. Scientists have uncovered around 150 species of animals, algae, and bacteria. What's amazing is that 98% of these species were soft-bodied creatures that don't usually fossilize well. They're preserved so spectacularly because they were probably buried rapidly by an underwater mudflow.

Aysheaia was a lobopod, which is a close relative of today's velvet worms, water bears (tardigrades), and arthropods, such as crabs. It lived alongside sponges.

Originally scientists thought **Hallucigenia** had a row of tentacles along its back and walked on spikes. But later they found that the spikes go on the back and it actually had two rows of legs.

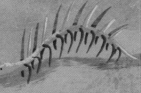

Many specimens of the arthropod **Marrella** have a dark stain that is high in copper. It might be blood!

Scientists know that the worm **Ottoia** was both a predator and a scavenger. They have found one with its last meal preserved in its gut and others eating a carcass.

Several specimens of **Waptia** have been discovered with up to 24 eggs attached to the underside of their headshields. This suggests this shrimplike arthropod cared for its young.

Anomalocaris was the largest predator in the Cambrian. It used its two front appendages to catch prey and popped its food into a circular-shaped mouth.

Opabinia was a bizarre arthropod with five stalked eyes and a long "nozzle" that ended in claws. It used this to catch prey.

Possibly a very early ancestor of vertebrates (animals with a backbone), **Pikaia** was an eel-like animal with no eyes. It used small feelers to find food in the mud.

Wiwaxia was a sluglike animal covered in leaf-shaped scales and spines. Sometimes their armor shows signs of damage, indicating they may have been attacked by a predator.

Echmatocrinus is thought to be an early echinoderm, belonging to the group that includes sea stars and urchins. It attached itself to the seafloor and used its arms to transport food to its mouth.

THE KING OF THE TRILOBITES

Dr. David Rudkin was on the hunt. The year was 1998 and the paleontologist (that's someone who studies fossils) was visiting a site known for fossils from the **Ordovician**—roughly 445 million years ago. He was looking for tracks left by trilobites, marine arthropods that were common back then. Large trilobite fossils had been found before in the area, but they were rare. David knew he had a better chance of finding their tracks, which were often bigger.

David was scrambling around rock ledges during low tide along the Hudson Bay coast in Manitoba, Canada. After stopping to take a closer look at something, he noticed he was literally stepping on the exposed portion of a fossil! He immediately realized he had found something special.

Removing the specimen was difficult. David and his team were in a race against the ocean. They had only about an hour and a half before the tide came in and submerged the fossil!

They were not prepared for a large excavation either, but they managed to get the specimen out... in a few pieces. After some work, the trilobite was found to be almost complete, only missing a little part of its tail. The team were stunned by how big it was. It was **GIGANTIC**—about the size of a pillow.

The team called the king of the trilobites **Isotelus rex**. It was the largest trilobite ever found! But who knows how many other giant trilobite fossils are hiding beneath the tides, waiting to be discovered...

Isotelus rex was seven times larger than an average trilobite.

SECRETS OF THE FOSSILS

Most of the time paleontologists handle fossils with extreme delicacy. Other times, cutting or drilling into fossils can tell us a lot more about them. But the fossils from a site in Herefordshire in the United Kingdom have to be **totally destroyed** to see how amazing they are! The Herefordshire fossils are preserved in breathtaking detail in 3D. However, it took over 150 years for scientists to figure that out, because the fossils are hidden inside hard, rocky structures called concretions.

Unbroken concretions

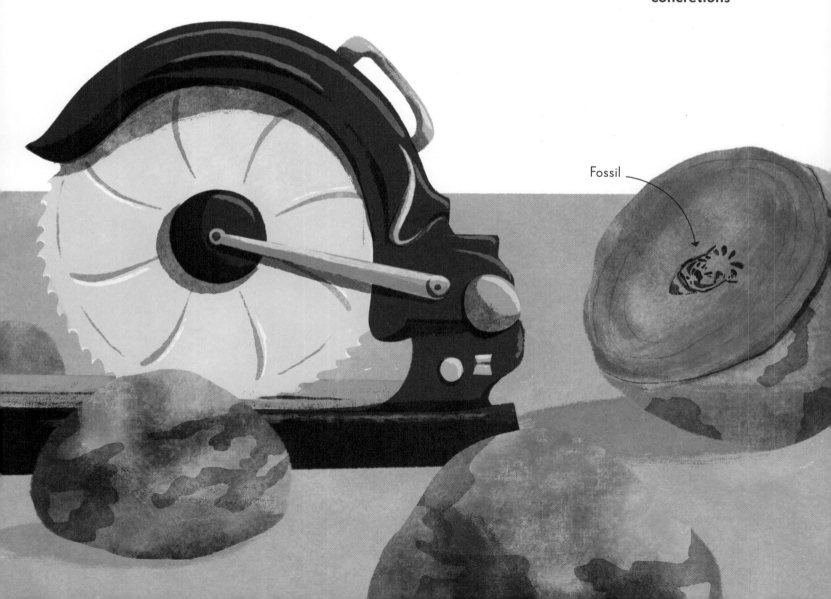

Fossil

To see the amazing fossils, the concretions are first split open in the lab. Around half of them will contain a fossil. Then the concretions are trimmed with a rock saw and mounted on a special slide. Specimens are ground down to less than the thickness of a human hair before being photographed. This process is repeated hundreds of times until the entire specimen has been sliced up and uploaded onto a computer. At this point the original specimen has **turned to dust**, but a digital fossil is reconstructed by combining the sections together using computers.

From these virtual fossils, paleontologists have discovered over 30 species, including sponges, worms, and mollusks. About 430 million years ago, these critters were living in a shallow subtropical sea that was south of the equator. They probably spent their time in deep, dark water roughly 330–660 ft (100–200 m) down. Out of 3,670 specimens, over a quarter of them are **arthropods**, related to modern animals like crabs and spiders. One arthropod, called Aquilonifer, used a long thread to carry its babies. Another, named Enalikter, didn't have eyes and had two pairs of spikes at the end of its tail.

At some point volcanic ash buried the animals in mud on the seafloor. Hard concretions formed and stopped the fossils from being squished, preserving them perfectly for us to study in the future!

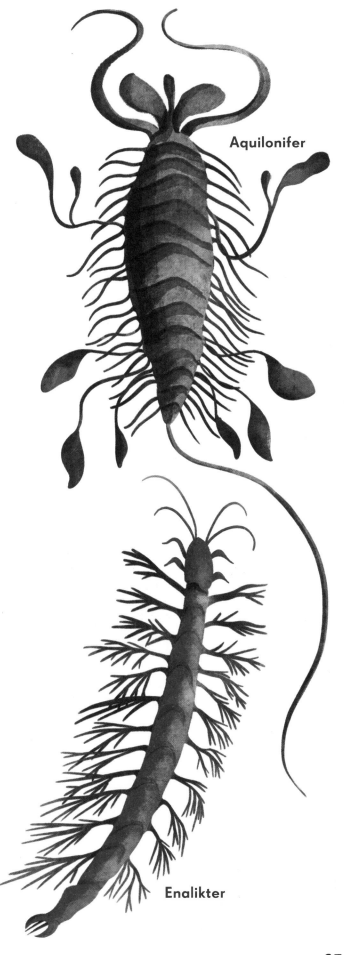

Aquilonifer

Enalikter

THE AGE OF ARMORED FISH

The Devonian (419–359 million years ago) is known as the Age of Fishes. Many fish groups appeared for the first time, including sharks and the ancestors of salmon. Two other groups—the Ostracoderms and Placoderms—developed bony plating around their heads, bodies, and fins. The oceans were battlegrounds and this armor was needed for protection!

Materpiscis gave birth to live young.

Entelognathus is the oldest known fish with a modern jaw. It was discovered in China and is 419 million years old.

Dunkleosteus is thought to be the first "superpredator." It had one of the most powerful bites ever.

Placoderms

These armored fish had jaws and lived in both freshwater and ocean environments. While most were active predators, some ate small plants called algae or fed on tiny creatures called plankton, in a similar way to modern basking sharks. Fossils from this group have been found on every continent.

Lunaspis was found in 400-million-year-old rocks in Germany, China, and Australia.

Brindabellaspis was an odd fish with a platypus-like snout.

Devonian map

At the start of the Devonian, plants had finally moved onto land. They were leafless and small, growing only 2 in (6 cm) tall. But by 370 million years ago, there were forests containing trees that could grow as high as 100 ft (30 m). Armored fish dominated in the water—until they went extinct due to climate change and competition from other animals.

Hemicyclaspis had sensory pores on its shovel-shaped headshield. These may have helped it navigate in murky water.

The mouth of **Doryaspis** was located near its eyes, just above the dart-like plate sticking out from its head.

Boreaspis may have used its long snout to stir up mud to find food. It lived in lagoons.

Lungmenshanaspis had a large hole in its head, which helped it smell and breathe.

Ostracoderms

This group of armored fish were jawless, meaning they couldn't chew! Without jaws they probably swam through the water with their mouths open, feeding on algae or small animals near the bottom. They were mostly small fish—the largest was only 24 in (60 cm) long.

THE WALKING FISH

At some point in history animals made their way from the ocean to the land. Because of this, paleontologists thought that animals with a mix of the features of fish and four-legged animals (tetrapods) must have existed at some point. They just needed to find one...

The paleontologists pinpointed the rough time period when they thought these transitional animals must have been alive. Then they searched for rocks of the right age and type that were exposed at the surface—with no pesky plants to get in the way. There was one place in the **Canadian Arctic** that ticked all these boxes.

The dig site

The team, led by Dr. Neil Shubin, a professor at the University of Chicago, were dropped into the wilderness by a helicopter for the first time in July 1999. They had only a small window of a few weeks before it started snowing again. They made the most of it. It helped that they were so far north—there were 24 hours of daylight in which they could work!

It would take searching the rocks every July until 2004 to find what they were looking for: the **V-shaped tip of a snout**. They encased it in a plaster jacket and took it away to be studied. After a year and a half of preparation came the exciting moment. They had discovered an almost complete fish with tetrapod features!

Nicknamed **"fishapod,"** this animal had fins, scales, and gills like a fish. It also had lungs, a flat head, a neck, and limb bones that looked very similar to all modern tetrapods. The local Inuit people named the fossil Tiktaalik, which in the native language means "large freshwater fish." Since the initial discovery the team has found more than 20 Tiktaalik individuals of all ages and sizes, some up to 9 ft (2.7 m) long.

Researchers think Tiktaalik was a predator that lived in shallow water, probably a **marshy swamp near the equator**, around 375 million years ago. It was able to swim, could prop itself up in a push-up position, and may have even been able to awkwardly waddle across mudflats.

MEET THE
GIANT BUGS

During the Carboniferous and Permian, arthropods—including insects and scorpions—reached gigantic sizes. At the time, oxygen levels in the atmosphere were around 30%, compared to 21% today. These oxygen levels allowed bugs to grow and grow. How would you feel if you came face-to-face with some of these critters?

The griffinfly **Meganeura** was one of the first insects with wings, making it one of the first flying creatures on Earth!

Mazothairos is sometimes called the "six-winged insect" because it had a set of mini winglets in front of its first pair of wings. It also had piercing mouthparts, possibly to drink plant fluids.

The millipede **Arthropleura** was the largest land invertebrate (animal without a backbone) of all time. Scientists think it ate plant debris from the forest floor.

Brodia is an arthropod that has been found in the United Kingdom and Canada. Some fossils have dark stripes preserved on the wings.

Xenoblatta is possibly the world's largest known cockroach-like insect! The specimen was discovered in a coal mine in Ohio.

Fossils of the giant scorpion **Pulmonoscorpius** were found in Scotland. Paleontologists aren't totally sure what it ate, but they think it was carnivorous (a meat-eater).

THE MYSTERY OF THE BUZZSAW SHARK

Around 1898, schoolchildren in Russia told their teacher about some **odd spiral fossils** that were found at the local rock quarry (you may have gathered by this point that quarries are great places to find fossils). The teacher passed on the information to the school inspector, Mr. Bessonov, who stopped by the quarry out of curiosity.

Mr. Bessonov sent the fossils to the director of the Russian Geological Survey, Alexander Karpinsky. He figured out that they were from **a shark from the Permian**, and were probably some kind of teeth... but where on the shark did they go?

This mystery would last more than 100 years. Then in 2013 the world finally got a clearer picture of the shark, which had been named **Helicoprion**, when a team from the United States scanned the spirals. Surprisingly, they found preserved cartilage from the upper and lower jaws. This showed that the spiral sat vertically in the middle of the shark's jaw—like a circular-saw blade! A student named Jesse Pruitt created a 3D model of the jaws and teeth to show how they fitted together. With this model they were able to tell what the shark liked to eat: soft-bodied prey, including squid-like belemnites, and shelled creatures called ammonites.

Karpinsky originally thought the upper jaw rolled up. He was wrong!

THE FAMILY IN THE BURROW

The Karoo Basin in South Africa is a vast, dry area surrounded by tall mountains and high plateaus. The rocks here record a 120-million-year-long span of Earth's history, from about 300 to 180 million years ago. And to the delight of paleontologists, they are full of fossils.

One group of rocks, known as the Beaufort, is especially fossiliferous. Over the years 30,000 vertebrate fossils have been collected (*vertebrate* means animals with backbones). It's one of the best places in the world to collect and study **synapsids**, a group of animals that includes mammals and their closest fossil relatives. Scientists are able to track the evolution of these animals through time and learn about their behavior.

In 1995, Dr. Roger M. H. Smith of the Iziko South African Museum was fossil hunting in a greenish-gray mudstone, a type of rock that once upon a time was mud. It was 260 million years old.

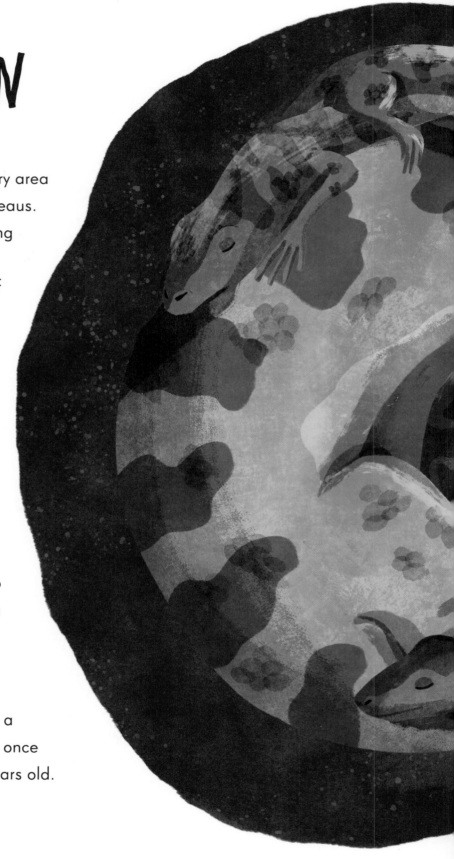

He stumbled across what he thought was the skeleton of a common type of Karoo synapsid, known as a therapsid. He didn't think much of it, so the specimen was never studied in detail.

Then, in the mid-2000s, Dr. Jennifer Botha-Brink decided to take another look at the specimen. And she was in for a surprise—her team uncovered not one but **five skeletons!** One of the skeletons was about 50% larger than the other smaller four. Can you guess why this might have been? Jennifer had an idea—she thought that the fossils were a family group made up of a parent and four babies. It was one of the oldest examples of a land vertebrate looking after its young in the fossil record. The group might have died in a burrow, either from a surprise flood or because of a collapse.

There were more surprises to come. The animals weren't therapsids after all. They turned out to be a rare, small lizard-like species called **Heleosaurus**. This story goes to show that it's always worth taking a second look at your discoveries!

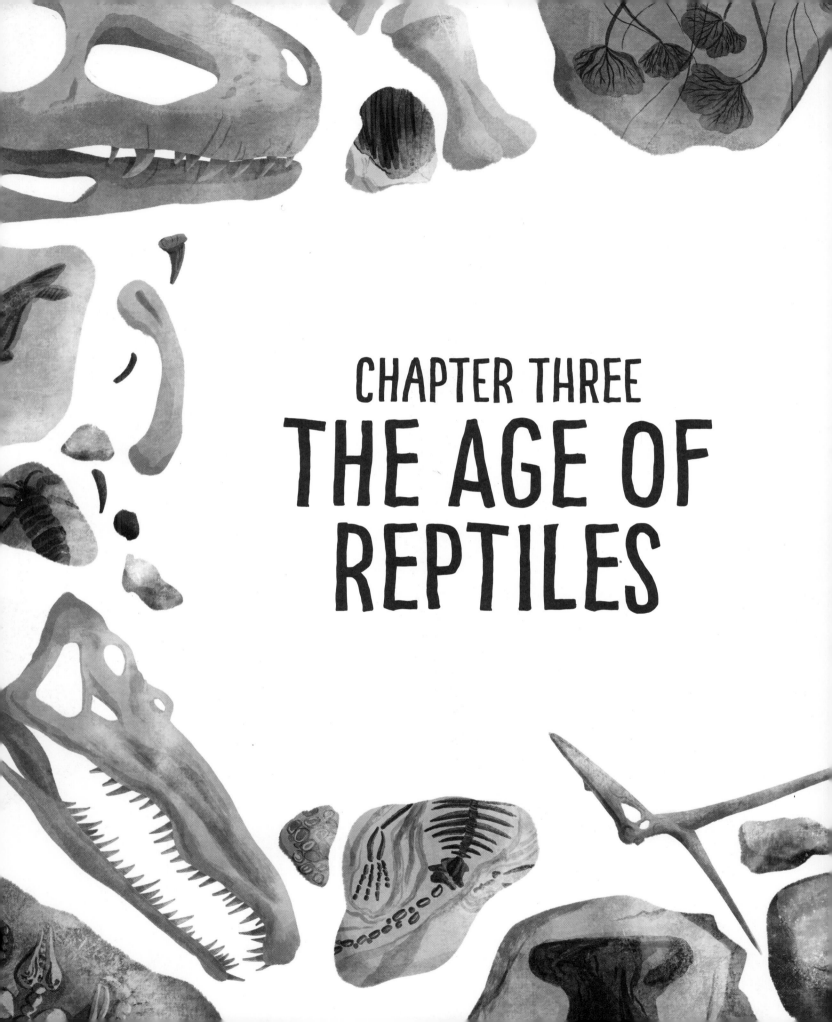

CHAPTER THREE
THE AGE OF REPTILES

The Mesozoic lasted from 252 to 66 million years ago. At the start of the period reptiles, like the crocodile-like phytosaurs, were dominant, while dinosaurs were small and rare. It wouldn't be until the Jurassic that dinosaurs began to rule the Earth. During this time birds and mammals also evolved. They would flourish after the dinosaurs met an unfortunate end...

THE SUPERCONTINENT OF
PANGAEA

Have you ever noticed how South America and Africa look like puzzle pieces that would fit together? Well, they did! Earth was once dominated by the supercontinent Pangaea. Some of the main pieces of evidence for Pangaea are fossils. Several species have been found on very different continents today, suggesting that these land masses were once joined.

Lystrosaurus

This dog-sized animal was one of the few survivors of the extinction event at the end of the Permian. It was very common in the early Triassic. Fossils have been found in Africa, India, and Antarctica.

Cynognathus

Fossils of this predator have been found in South America and Africa. It was just over 3 ft (1 m) long and closely related to mammals. Dimples on the skull suggest it might have had whiskers.

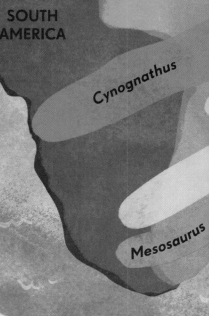

NORTH
AMERICA

AFRICA

SOUTH
AMERICA

Cynognathus

Mesosaurus

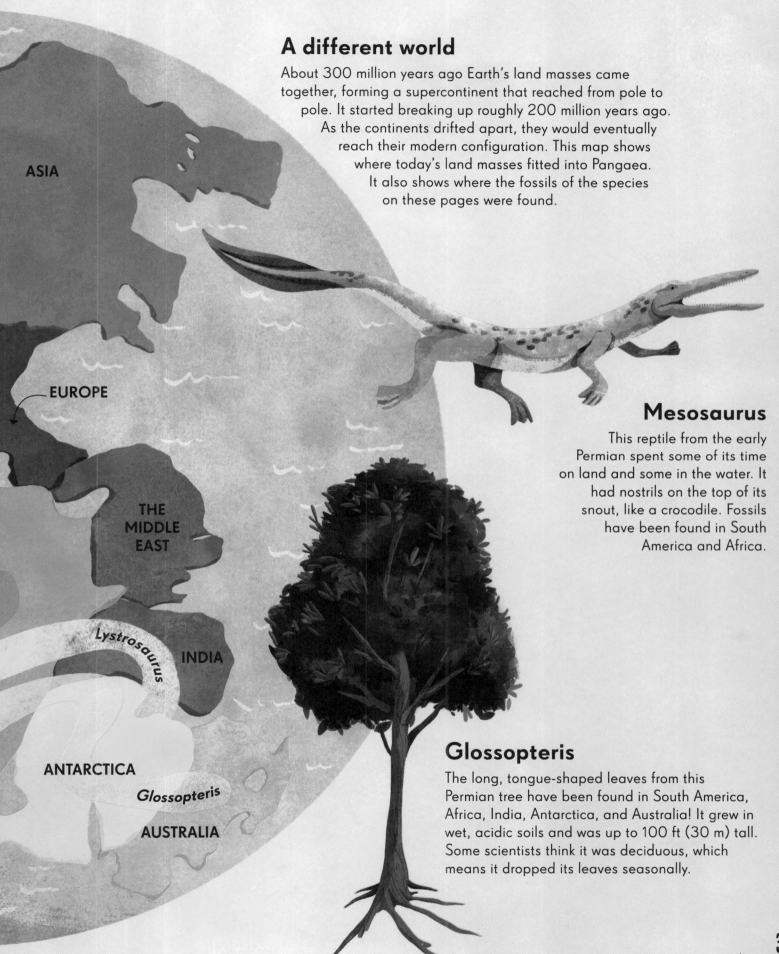

A different world

About 300 million years ago Earth's land masses came together, forming a supercontinent that reached from pole to pole. It started breaking up roughly 200 million years ago. As the continents drifted apart, they would eventually reach their modern configuration. This map shows where today's land masses fitted into Pangaea. It also shows where the fossils of the species on these pages were found.

ASIA

EUROPE

THE MIDDLE EAST

Lystrosaurus

INDIA

ANTARCTICA

Glossopteris

AUSTRALIA

Mesosaurus

This reptile from the early Permian spent some of its time on land and some in the water. It had nostrils on the top of its snout, like a crocodile. Fossils have been found in South America and Africa.

Glossopteris

The long, tongue-shaped leaves from this Permian tree have been found in South America, Africa, India, Antarctica, and Australia! It grew in wet, acidic soils and was up to 100 ft (30 m) tall. Some scientists think it was deciduous, which means it dropped its leaves seasonally.

THE TRIASSIC FOOTPRINTS

Prorotodactylus footprint

In 1980, a year after construction started on a dam in Poland, paleontologist Tadeusz Ptaszyński found three unusual slabs of rock. On them were fossil footprints! And they weren't alone—during the following years, tons and tons of fossil footprints were collected.

Out of the roughly 3,500 individual footprints, a few were made by the earliest **dinosauromorphs**. I know what you're thinking—*what's a dinosauromorph? A dinosaur that can morph into other dinosaurs?* Well, I'm afraid not. These weren't actually dinosaurs. They were close relatives, known as proto-dinosaurs. Some of the footprints, from an animal called Prorotodactylus, were about 250 million years old. And they revealed fascinating secrets of the past.

Based on the ancient imprints, researchers were able to reconstruct what the animal that made them might have looked like. Prorotodactylus was cat-sized and walked on all fours. It held its legs directly under its body, not sprawled to the sides like a lizard. And when it was walking, only its toes touched the ground! Based on the big spaces between the footprints, its limbs must have been pretty long. And since the footprints went over the handprints, scientists think its legs would have been longer than its arms. So, all in all, poor Prorotodactylus was kind of an **awkward-looking animal**.

Another surprising thing was how rare the dinosauromorph tracks were compared to all of the other animal tracks preserved with them. This meant dinosaurs and their ancestors were minor players in their habitats when they first evolved. That, of course, would soon change...

WHAT EXACTLY IS A
DINOSAUR?

There have been around 1,000 species of dinosaur described since the word "dinosaur" (which means "terrible lizard") was coined in 1842. But what makes a dinosaur... a dinosaur? The main way to tell is by looking at its posture.

Stand up straight

Dinosaurs, like Stegosaurus, had an upright stance. They held their legs directly under their bodies, like mammals. Other reptiles, such as crocodiles, have a sprawling stance and walk with their legs out to the sides. We also know, from dinosaur footprints and skeletons, that dinosaurs did not drag their tails.

Crocodile

Stegosaurus

Egg-cellent parents

All dinosaurs laid and hatched from eggs. These eggs came in a variety of shapes and sizes. Giants like Titanosaurus had almost perfectly round eggs, while smaller dinosaurs like Oviraptor had eggs that were long and oval-shaped. The largest dinosaur eggs were more than 24 in (60 cm) long!

Gnashers

Although a few dinosaurs were toothless, most had teeth that were constantly replaced throughout their lives. Plant-eaters replaced teeth roughly every 56 days, while it could take T. rex up to two years!

The pubis bone (yellow) points forward in Saurischian dinosaurs.

In Ornithischian dinosaurs, the pubis bone (yellow) points backward.

The hips don't lie

Dinosaurs can be split into two main groups: Saurischians and Ornithischians. The way to tell them apart is by looking at their hips.

Dinosaurs in the park

Believe it or not, birds evolved from a line of dinosaurs around 150 million years ago. That means that birds are dinosaurs! We now call the dinosaurs that went extinct 66 million years ago "non-avian dinosaurs" to distinguish them from birds.

THE RANCHER'S DELIGHT

In the 1960s, a local rancher and artist named Victorino Herrera was wandering through the remote, rocky terrain of northwest Argentina when he suddenly froze. There, in front of him, were **bones** sticking out of the rock face. Excited by his discovery, he made his way back home before contacting the famous Argentinian paleontologists Osvaldo Reig and José Bonaparte. Together, they rapidly made their way back to the site.

It turned out to be a treasure trove! The team collected many fossils, including the back half of what looked like a dinosaur. Osvaldo named it **Herrerasaurus** in honor of the rancher. A few years later, in 1988, an expedition that included Victorino's nephew Dante Herrera found a complete skull of Herrerasaurus. It was a game-changer, confirming that Herrerasaurus was one of the earliest known dinosaurs—a whopping 231 million years old!

Herrerasaurus was a carnivore (meat-eater) that walked on two legs. It was huge, but it wasn't the biggest predator around... That title belonged to the **Saurosuchus**, a crocodile-like giant that enjoyed nothing more than snacking on early dinosaurs— like our good friend Herrerasaurus.

Herrerasaurus
skull

RULERS OF THE
TRIASSIC

For most of the Triassic, dinosaurs were a minor part of the ecosystem. The land was instead dominated by the survivors of the most recent extinction—animals such as therapsids (some of which would evolve into mammals) and reptiles. And while some of these creatures may look like dinosaurs, none of them are!

Cynodonts were relatives of mammals that probably laid eggs, but they were warm-blooded and had fur.

Phytosaurs were reptiles very similar to modern crocodiles, but there were some differences. Their nostrils were located near their eyes on the top of their heads and they had serrated teeth, like the edge of a steak knife.

Temnospondyls were amphibians that had large, flat heads that looked kind of like toilet seats. One species, Metoposaurus, was 10 ft (3 m) long.

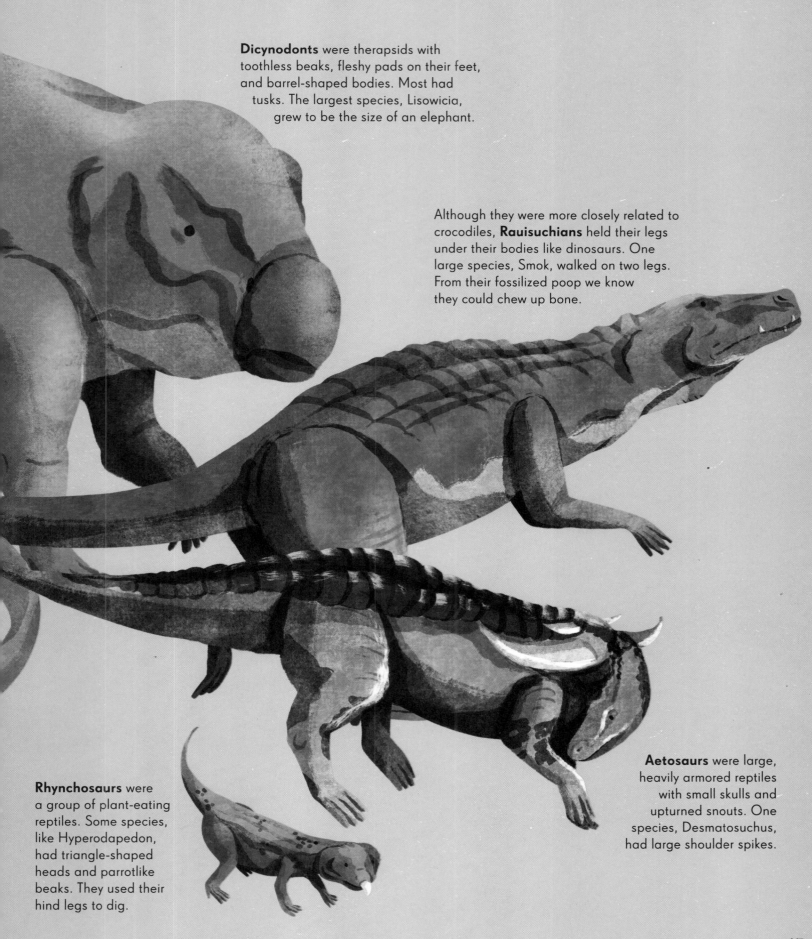

Dicynodonts were therapsids with toothless beaks, fleshy pads on their feet, and barrel-shaped bodies. Most had tusks. The largest species, Lisowicia, grew to be the size of an elephant.

Although they were more closely related to crocodiles, **Rauisuchians** held their legs under their bodies like dinosaurs. One large species, Smok, walked on two legs. From their fossilized poop we know they could chew up bone.

Aetosaurs were large, heavily armored reptiles with small skulls and upturned snouts. One species, Desmatosuchus, had large shoulder spikes.

Rhynchosaurs were a group of plant-eating reptiles. Some species, like Hyperodapedon, had triangle-shaped heads and parrotlike beaks. They used their hind legs to dig.

THE BABY-EATERS

It wasn't just raining, it was pouring. It was 220 million years ago, during the Triassic period, in what is now New Mexico. Running through the storm were a herd of **Coelophysis**, some of the earliest known dinosaurs. In their panic they tripped over one another as floodwater lapped around their feet.

Fast-forward to the 20th century and 30 large blocks of fossils were removed from a quarry. Inside the blocks were an estimated 2,850 Coelophysis skeletons. And they had a story to tell...

The skeletons ranged from hatchlings to fully grown adults, and they were usually found tangled together. A researcher was looking at two adult specimens when he noticed something unusual—there appeared to be baby Coelophysis bones where the stomach of one of the adults was. Could the adults have eaten babies?!

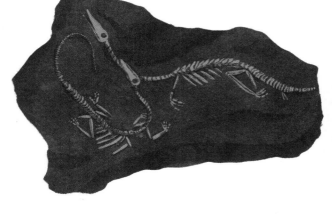

The scientist also realized that thousands of Coelophysis had died at the same time, possibly in a flash flood. After being caught by the rising waters their bodies might have floated into a lake, where they were eventually buried in sediment.

A few years later, researchers took another look at the two adults in an attempt to solve the mystery of the baby bones. The ribs of one of the adults were pulled back—possibly from the **body exploding** after death—making it nearly impossible to tell if any of the bones were originally in the stomach. The other skeleton did have some bones in its stomach, but they were from an extinct crocodile relative, not a baby Coelophysis. It seemed like the mystery had been solved.

Then, in 2009, paleontologists investigated a different, fairly complete Coelophysis specimen. They noticed a cololite, a block of digested food that had not yet become a coprolite (**fossilised poop**—yes, that's a thing). Inside the cololite were the hands and feet of, you guessed it, baby Coelophysis! And there was also a skull with preserved vomit nearby that had baby Coelophysis jaws in it. So it looks like Coelophysis were **cannibals** after all!

THE FIRST GIANTS

Sauropods, including famous dinosaurs like Diplodocus and Brachiosaurus, were the largest land animals ever. Some were **as long as a jumbo jet** and a few shattered the scales at 65 tons! The earliest sauropods, called sauropodomorphs, appeared with the first dinosaurs around 230 million years ago. At first they were small, only about as long as a motorcycle, and they walked on two legs. So when did sauropods get so big?

At first paleontologists believed huge sauropods appeared in the Jurassic period, around 180 million years ago. But that changed in 2018, with a startling discovery in northwest Argentina.

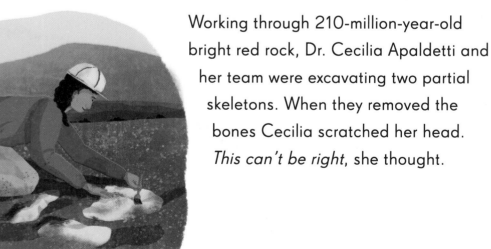

Working through 210-million-year-old bright red rock, Dr. Cecilia Apaldetti and her team were excavating two partial skeletons. When they removed the bones Cecilia scratched her head. *This can't be right*, she thought.

The dinosaur they had discovered, **Ingentia**, was roughly three times the size of the other Triassic dinosaurs. But Cecilia noted it definitely wasn't one of the later sauropods—it had a shorter neck and its legs were more bendy. Excited, the team got to work finding out all they could about this gargantuan animal.

First they needed to find out how the animal grew. To do this they carefully sawed out a super-thin slice of bone (don't worry, the dinosaur was already dead). By analyzing the structure of the bone under a microscope they could see that Ingentia had **growth spurts**, unlike later sauropods which grew almost continuously. There were bursts of rapid growth followed by little to no growth, similar to the way trees grow.

But while Ingentia grew differently, it might have breathed the same way as its larger relatives. The team discovered holes in its backbone that would have housed air sacs. These were part of a breathing system, like that used by birds. It meant Ingentia was able to get twice the amount of oxygen from a single deep breath. The air sacs also helped keep the dinosaur cool and made its skeleton weigh less—all incredible adaptations that helped this early giant grow!

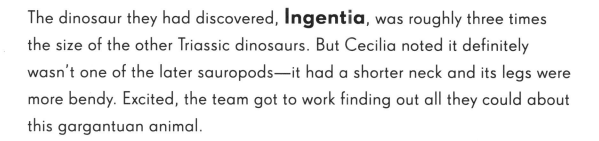

Ingentia had air sacs attached to its spine that helped it breathe efficiently.

WEIRD LIFE OF
THE TRIASSIC

The Triassic was an odd time. It started after the largest mass extinction of all time and ended in another extinction. Life had about 50 million years to recover, only to be almost completely wiped out again! This is why a lot of life in the Triassic seems so... well, weird.

Sharovipteryx was a small lizard with thin membranes attached to its legs. It's thought these animals glided from tree to tree using these "wings."

Erythrosuchus was the largest predator in the early Triassic. It had a big head attached to a crocodile-like body.

Atopodentatus was an early marine reptile. It had a hammer-shaped mouth and a bunch of comblike teeth, which it used to gather plants from the seafloor.

Shonisaurus was a type of reptile called an ichthyosaur. It was the largest marine reptile ever—the size of a modern fin whale! It's thought that the juveniles had teeth, but the adults were toothless. Like dolphins, they lived in groups called pods.

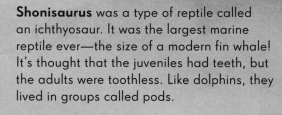

Known as the "monkey reptile," **Drepanosaurus** climbed trees and had claws on the end of its tail.

Shringasaurus was a reptile that used its long neck to browse higher than other plant-eaters.

The most notable feature of the reptile **Longisquama** was the plume of long scales on its back. Scientists think they may have been used to impress potential mates.

Tanystropheus was the giraffe of the ocean. It had an extremely long neck—it was half the length of the animal! It used this to catch fish and squid.

THE 3D PTEROSAUR

Pterosaurs, like the famous Pterodactyl, terrorized the skies of the Mesozoic. And although they lived at the same time as dinosaurs, they weren't dinosaurs but **flying reptiles**. Finding pterosaur bones is difficult—they're very delicate and are almost always destroyed during fossilization.

Caelestiventus skull

Dr. Brooks Britt and Dr. Fabio M. Dalla Vecchia were hunting for bones in Utah, well known for its dinosaur discoveries. When the team spotted a pterosaur bone poking out of a rock they knew they had come across something special.

Now was the tricky part. Since the bones were too fragile to remove completely from the rock, the paleontologists had to cut out a block of rock to take back to the lab. Then they had a great idea: They decided to **X-ray** it. What they found took their breath away. Instead of being crushed like most pterosaur fossils, this pterosaur had been preserved in 3D! They called it Caelestiventus, and promptly printed out a model of it using a 3D printer.

From the model they discovered that this 210-million-year-old was much larger than other Triassic pterosaurs. It also had a hornlike crest and a pelican-like throat pouch. Unlike pelicans, however, Caelestiventus lived around a lake surrounded by sand dunes in a giant desert, and there's no evidence there were fish nearby. So this pterosaur probably spent its time hunting small reptiles.

THE FROZEN REPTILE

Searching for dinosaurs in Antarctica is not easy, and that's putting it mildly. Firstly, in case you hadn't noticed, Antarctica is covered in snow and ice! That means paleontologists can only hunt for fossils on the tops of mountains that poke through the thick ice. This didn't deter geologist David Elliot. In 1991, at an altitude of 13,000 ft (4,000 m), a mere snowball's throw from the South Pole, he discovered the bones of a dinosaur that would later be called **Cryolophosaurus**.

If finding the fossil was difficult, excavating it was even harder. It took three weeks, and the team had to use power tools such as jackhammers and rock saws to remove large blocks of rock. Oh, and then the blocks had to be flown off the mountain by helicopters. Was all this effort worth it? You bet.

Antarctica was a very different place in the early Jurassic. It was farther north and had a cool climate that supported forests. These forests contained trees with tongue-shaped leaves, which were chomped

up by Glacialisaurus, an early relative of the sauropods. Shuffling around the feet of these large dinosaurs were tritylodonts, close relatives of mammals. And soaring majestically above were flocks of pterosaurs.

Cryolophosaurus was a big theropod (part of T. rex's family) and a top predator. It could hunt large prey, like Glacialisaurus, but it was probably an **opportunistic predator**—which means it wasn't picky and would eat whatever it could! Cryolophosaurus had a prominent crest above its eyes, which may have been used to help individuals identify each other or as an impressive display. Who would have thought this ruler of the Jurassic would have ended up frozen in ice at the top of a mountain?

MARY ANNING: FOSSIL HUNTER

Have you ever heard the tongue twister "She sells seashells by the seashore"? It was inspired by Mary Anning. Mary was born on May 21, 1799, in Lyme Regis, England. Her family was very poor, and Mary **sold fossils** that she found in the nearby sea cliffs to make money. With her trusty dog Tray at her side, she collected fossils that were between 190 and 200 million years old.

Mary's paleontology career started early. When she was 12, she excavated a 16-ft-long (5-m-long) skeleton, after her brother Joseph had found the skull. She sold the specimen for what would be equal to roughly $700 in today's money. It was an extinct marine reptile called an ichthyosaur (the first of its kind announced!) and it was named Temnodontosaurus. But this was just her first incredible discovery...

In 1823, Mary found a type of long-necked marine reptile called Plesiosaurus. And then the finds kept coming! Dimorphodon, the first British pterosaur, was discovered by Mary in 1828. That same year she also identified fossilized ink in squid-like creatures called belemnites. To top it all off, in 1829 she worked with the scientist William Buckland to coin the term **coprolite** for fossilized poop.

Temnodontosaurus skull

Temnodontosaurus in better times

Mary's fossils are still being used to this day. In 2015, a new species of Ichthyosaurus was named in her honor. Scientists had used several specimens to describe the new creature, one of which had been collected by Mary.

Though she had no formal education, Mary taught herself geology and biology and made detailed specimen drawings by candlelight. Many prominent scientists of the day visited her shop, **Anning's Fossil Depot,** to see her finds. Unfortunately, during her life she was rarely credited for her many discoveries, but today she is celebrated as one of the most famous paleontologists of all time!

THE MEGARAFT

Once upon a time, something epic was drifting through the prehistoric oceans. On board were alien-like life-forms called **Seirocrinus**. They had a flowerlike head and a long stem. They were part of a family called the crinoids, a group that dates all the way back to the Cambrian. But these remarkable organisms weren't plants—they were marine animals!

Young crinoids swam around until they found the perfect spot to anchor themselves permanently to a surface, usually the seafloor. There, they would use feathery arms to filter tiny pieces of food from the water. But in 1908 scientists found evidence that Seirocrinus behaved very differently.

A massive specimen was unearthed in Germany. It was so big it took 18 years to study! The slab contained a piece of driftwood with 280 Seirocrinus individuals attached to its underside. Some had stems a whopping 65 ft (20 m) long. They would have dangled beneath the log, resembling a **humongous jellyfish**.

The reason why these crinoids adopted the floating-log lifestyle might also be why they were so well preserved. They lived 182 million years ago, when an event left the bottoms of the oceans with no oxygen. This meant that crinoids couldn't attach to the seafloor, but it also meant that bacteria or scavengers couldn't destroy the valuable specimen. In 2020, a group of researchers used the spectacular fossil to figure out how long one of these raft colonies could stay afloat. They imagined this log might have sailed the oceans for 20 years!

THE MISSING BONES

In 2005, a group of scientists from Germany, led by Dr. Ulrich Joger, traveled to the Republic of Niger in West Africa. They were looking for dinosaur bones. The local Tuareg people told the team about an area with lots of fossils in the Niger desert, so the team trekked to the hot and remote area. Sure enough, once they arrived they found pieces of weathered bone all over the ground.

They started digging around and uncovered an **almost complete dinosaur spine**, curled in a circle. It was HUGE and, by the looks of it, from a medium-sized sauropod. However, the team didn't have the tools or the permits they needed to excavate. So they hastily reburied the skeleton to protect it.

The next year Ulrich received permission to return to the site and remove the bones. He made a trip to the site in November and found the skeleton just as they'd left it—good news. The following March the team headed back to the desert. Five people drove the long way with the gear—a 20-day trip all the way from Germany.

When they finally got to the site they quickly noticed something was wrong. The skeleton was **nowhere to be found**. This was bad news. It looked like it had been professionally excavated before they had got there. Devastated, the team scrambled to find another dinosaur to dig up.

Luckily, not too far away they found another skeleton, and it even appeared to be the same kind of dinosaur. After carefully removing all of the bones, the team sent them back to Germany. It took two and a half years back at the lab to prepare the specimen. To the team's delight, they found it was a new species! They named it **Spinophorosaurus**. Unfortunately their specimen was only about 70% complete, but they got word that there was a similar specimen housed in Spain. They took a look and, to their shock, realized it was the missing skeleton! It turned out a crew from a museum in Spain had excavated it when they were away. Using the two animals, the scientists were able to build a more complete picture of the spectacular dinosaur.

DINO DEATH TRAP

Between 2001 and 2006, paleontologists found three bone beds in China that were pretty strange. Bone beds are usually horizontal, with bones scattered across the surface. But these were vertical! The bones of small animals, including dinosaurs, were **stacked on top of one another** in pits that were about 3–6 ft (1–2 m) wide and deep. The rock inside the pits was formed from a mixture of mud, sand, and volcanic ash. It was a head-scratcher. But then the scientists came up with a theory. Here's what they think happened...

Around 160 million years ago, volcanic eruptions blanketed a wetland, creating a hard crust over the muddy marsh. A large sauropod, maybe a Mamenchisaurus, walked through. As the dinosaur moved, its gigantic size made it sink deep into the mud. With each step, water and mud quickly filled in the footprints—**creating traps**.

The area was home to many small, feathered dinosaurs that were light enough to walk across the crust without it breaking. However, one wrong step would send them **tumbling into the footprint pit!** And once they fell in, it was very hard to get out. One pit contained five skeletons from three different dinosaurs, including Guanlong, a small relative of T. rex. The sauropod probably didn't realize the carnage it had caused!

FLIGHT, FUZZ, AND
FEATHERS

It is really hard to tell when birdlike dinosaurs evolved into birds because they share many features, such as hollow bones. Many non-birds have been found with a feathery or fuzzy body—and some could fly!

Archaeopteryx is thought to be the oldest known bird. However, some paleontologists think it was still just a dinosaur.

Birds

Birds appear in the late Jurassic, around 150 million years ago. While many of the animals on these pages look like birds, only one is usually classified as a bird. Can you find it?

At 160 million years old, **Yi qi** is the oldest flying non-avian dinosaur. It had leathery, bat-like wings—and the shortest dinosaur name!

Kulindadromeus was covered in "dino fuzz." It had three types of scales on its arms, legs, and tail.

Preserved feathers show that the birdlike dinosaur **Caihong** was black with a brightly colored head.

Anchiornis was a four-winged dinosaur with leg feathers. It had a red head-crest and black and white stripes on its wings.

Bones

Pterosaurs, theropod dinosaurs, and birds all have hollow bones strengthened by internal struts. They are super light— handy if you want to fly!

Feathers

Feather-like structures have been found on dinosaurs and pterosaurs. This means feathers probably evolved before either of these groups did—in the early Triassic.

Hesperornithoides was a raptor-like dinosaur. It was covered in feathers but couldn't fly.

A fuzzy body covering has even been found on a currently unnamed pterosaur. It isn't a dinosaur or a bird! It's a flying reptile.

Early feathers had a single hollow filament known as **"dino fuzz."**

A tuft of filaments called **barbs** evolved next.

Then small branches called **barbules** appeared.

Barbs fused together to form a central shaft called the **rachis**.

Then the barbules developed **hooks**, holding the feather together.

67

THE SAD STORY OF BIG AL

The first Allosaurus fossil was discovered in 1869, but it wouldn't officially be named until 1877. And while many specimens of this Jurassic carnivore have been found since, it wasn't until 1991 that arguably the most famous Allosaurus was discovered. Scientists called it Big Al.

A group of scientists investigated the Big Al site in Wyoming. The fossil was about 145–150 million years old. Since the bones were already partially exposed and it was September, the crew had to work quickly before winter arrived. With the help of lots of volunteers, they finished the excavation in just eight days! Public tours to the site were organized. More than **4,000 people** made the trek out to see the dinosaur dig, including kids who were driven in on school buses.

It would take another two years to collect all the bones and three years to prepare them, but Big Al turned out to be about 95% complete— one of the most complete Allosaurus ever found! However, it was only 26 ft (8 m) long, though adults could reach 39 ft (12 m). So Big Al was not yet fully grown. It was also covered in signs of disease and had sustained injuries all over its body. One of the worst was an **infected toe bone** that would have caused poor Big Al to limp.

We don't know what caused all the injuries or exactly how Big Al died. But it was not a healthy dinosaur and would've struggled to find food and water. At some point it couldn't go on any longer. Big Al **collapsed on the bank of a river** and died. Part of its skeleton was eaten by beetles and scattered around by scavengers, no doubt delighted by a free meal. Eventually it was totally buried in sediment from the river and left to fossilize.

In life Big Al didn't have a great time, but these days this sad Allosaurus is a superstar!

THE BONE WARS

If you think paleontology has always been a noble profession, think again! In 1877, a bunch of extremely well-preserved dinosaur bones were found at three separate sites in Colorado and Wyoming. The people who found the bones quickly sent letters to the top paleontologists of the time—Othniel Charles Marsh and Edward Drinker Cope.

Othniel and Edward used to be good friends, but they had a falling-out in 1868 and a **30-year bitter rivalry** began. Those letters from 1877 were the start of the Bone Wars. Othniel and Edward battled each other to see who could find the greatest number of fossils and name the most new species.

**Othniel
Charles Marsh**

Stegosaurus

Apatosaurus

Neither Othniel nor Edward had any problems turning to the dark side. They spied on each other, attempted to bribe people, stole fossils, and even once got into a fight! Worst of all, when they were finished with a quarry they would **blow it up with dynamite**, hoping to destroy any fossils they might have missed so their competitor wouldn't find them. All of the fossils were collected on land that had recently been taken from indigenous people.

During the Bone Wars Edward discovered 56 new dinosaur species, while Othniel found 80. Many famous dinosaurs were discovered for the first time, including Stegosaurus, Apatosaurus, Camarasaurus, Dryptosaurus, and Nanosaurus. The Bone Wars had an impact on how paleontologists understood Jurassic life, how specimens were collected and displayed in museums, and how the public perceived paleontology. As for Othniel and Edward? Their rivalry left both of them nearly **bankrupt!**

Edward
Drinker Cope

Camarasaurus

Dryptosaurus

Nanosaurus

A TALE IN TWO PARTS

Sometimes in paleontology you need a bit of luck. In 1999 the front half of a brand-new type of stegosaur was discovered when a road was being built between two villages in Portugal. Unfortunately this wasn't before the back half had been destroyed! The skeleton was encased in sandstone that was roughly 150 million years old. It had an extremely long neck with at least 17 neck bones. In 2009, the stegosaur was named **Miragaia**.

Then, the same year, something amazing happened. Deep in a government agency vault, a back half of a Miragaia was discovered! What were the chances?

The specimen had been stored there for a long time. It hadn't been cleaned up, and it had no collection number or field notes. This made it hard to find out where it had been found (note to self—always label discoveries), but scientists reckoned it probably came from farmland in central Portugal.

In 2015, a scientist named Francisco Costa started investigating the rediscovered fossils. And since this second specimen had some bones that overlapped with the first one, paleontologists were able to reconstruct a fairly complete skeleton of Miragaia! Despite this, they were still not sure why the stegosaur had such a **long neck**. They had two theories—either it allowed Miragaia to browse for food higher than other animals in its habitat, or it was used as part of a mating display, like the long tail of a peacock.

THE BACK HALF WAS IN STORAGE FOR 60 YEARS.

THE FINAL SUPPER

Have you ever eaten something you wish you hadn't? Well, it probably wasn't as bad as the meal in this story...

During the Late Jurassic, Germany was a group of islands with **lagoons** at the edge of the ocean. The limestone that formed from the soft mud on the lagoon floor is full of amazing fossils, including the most famous specimen of Archaeopteryx, one of the first obvious links between dinosaurs and birds.

In 2009, a fossil from this limestone was discovered that told a dramatic story. It goes something like this: A small pterosaur named **Rhamphorhynchus** was flying above the lagoon looking for a snack. After spotting a school of fish it flew down very close to the water, so close its tail may have dragged across the surf. Then it opened its mouth and skimmed its lower jaw across the surface of the water.

It quickly snagged a fish—dinner was served! Alas, before it could fully swallow its supper, it was **rudely interrupted**. Suddenly, a much larger fish, called Aspidorhynchus, burst through the water! It stabbed through the leathery wing of Rhamphorhynchus with its spiked snout.

The Aspidorhynchus pulled the pterosaur down into the depths, causing it to drown. But at this point the large fish realized there was a problem. Its **upper jaw was stuck** in the pterosaur's wing! It tried everything to free itself— swimming rapidly around, shaking its head—but nothing worked. The weight of the Rhamphorhynchus (and its snack) made the exhausted larger fish sink down to the bottom of the lagoon where there was no oxygen. It died still tangled up with Rhamphorhynchus, the two destined to be forever entwined.

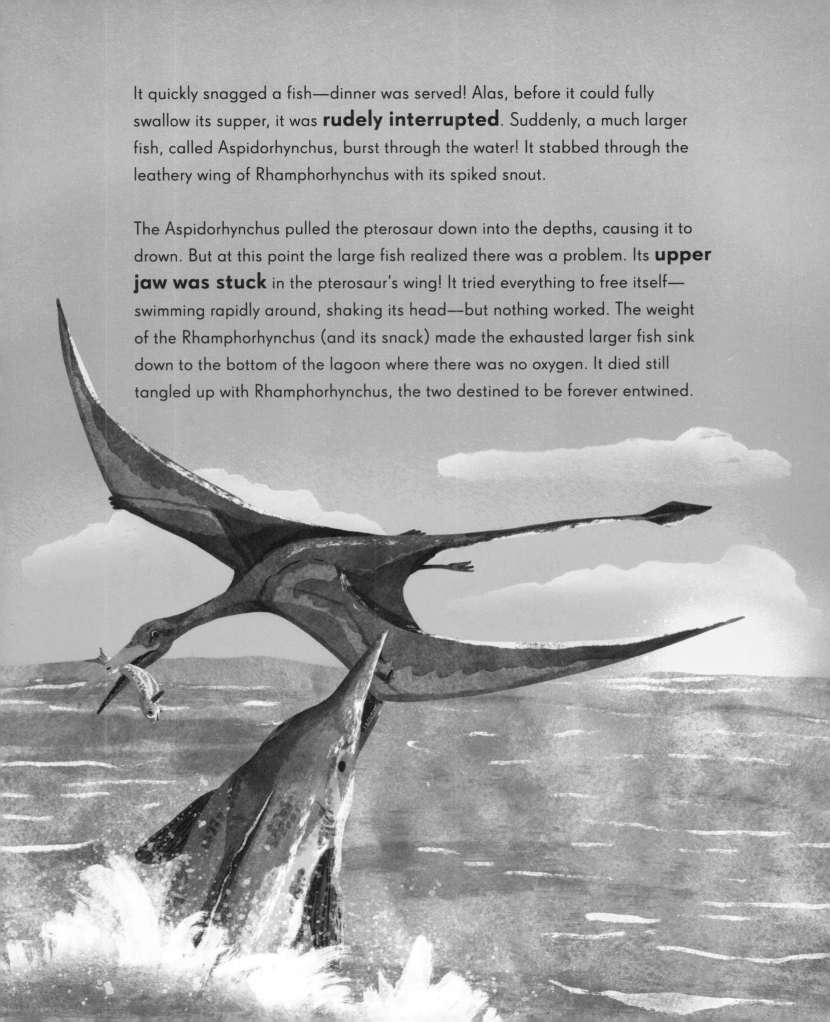

THE SECRETS OF THE MINE

Being a gravel miner is hard work. And sometimes, instead of digging up gravel, you stumble upon a dinosaur bone and the gravel pit is taken over by excited paleontologists! That's exactly what happened at Angeac-Charente in southwest France in 2008. And it turned out there wasn't just one bone—oh no—there were a LOT of fossils.

Excavations took place every summer for the next eight years. In that time a whopping **73,000 fossils** were uncovered! And they were made up of different types, including body fossils, such as teeth and bones, and trace fossils, such as coprolites (dinosaur poop) and footprints. In total, 3,123 were coprolites—that sure is a lot of ancient poop.

The fossils ranged from microscopic pollen grains from prehistoric plants to a giant sauropod leg bone. There was also a **mass death pit!** The bones of 44 ostrichlike dinosaurs had been heavily trampled, but scientists don't know how they died. Conditions in the swamp had made it a great environment for preserving fossils, including rare 4D footprints that magically revealed skin scales from lumbering sauropods.

With all of this information, paleontologists were able to imagine this part of France during the **early Cretaceous**, about 140 million years ago. Ferns and conifers were the major plants around, thriving in the humid, subtropical climate. There were crocodiles, turtles, and fish living in a freshwater swamp, while dinosaurs ruled the land. In the air, pterosaurs still dominated, but a new group of flying reptiles, including the now famous Archaeopteryx, were on the rise.

THE SPINY SAUROPOD

While some of the largest sauropods weighed almost as much as a space shuttle and stretched more than 130 ft (40 m) long, not all of them were that big. One group of sauropods had smaller bodies and shorter necks. And instead of bulk, a couple of members of this group relied on something unusual for protection.

A single, nearly complete Amargasaurus specimen was discovered in 1984. For a sauropod, it was very small—a mere 30 ft (9 m) long. But there was something more striking about it. Sticking out of its neck bones were **gigantic spikes!** These terrifying bony spines were lined in two rows down the back of the dinosaur's neck.

There's been a lot of speculation about what these spikes were for. They probably didn't poke through the dinosaur's skin. They were covered with keratin, kind of like a cow's horns. Some scientists have suggested they were draped in skin, forming a ginormous sail. Or maybe Amargasaurus had a hump, like a bison, behind the spikes? Some researchers even think that if Amargasaurus shook its neck, **it could make sounds** with the spines! The most common theory is that they were used for defense, possibly against meat-eating dinosaurs called Abelisauroids. What do you think the spikes were used for?

THE BEASTS OF
PREHISTORIC CHINA

Fossils from three different rock layers in northeast China are rather special. They include creatures and plants from an ancient ecosystem called the Jehol Biota. About 130–120 million years ago, there was a lot of volcanic activity in the region. Some scientists think these creatures were buried in a lake by ash from the eruptions, like what happened to the Roman town of Pompeii. As a result, the remains of the animals were perfectly preserved! Here are a few we've found so far.

Reptiles

Twenty-one species of pterosaur have been found in the Jehol Biota, including eggs containing babies! Scientists also discovered Xianglong—the only known fossilized gliding lizard. It used its ribs to soar between trees.

Xianglong

Tyrannopsylla

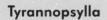

Mammals

Repenomamus was found with chunks of baby dinosaurs in its gut! The giant flea Tyrannopsylla may have lived in its fur.

Repenomamus

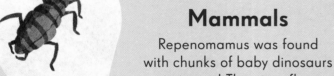

Sinosauropteryx

Dinosaurs

Yutyrannus was the largest dinosaur with feathers, Tianyulong had long feather-like filaments, and Sinosauropteryx had a striped tail!

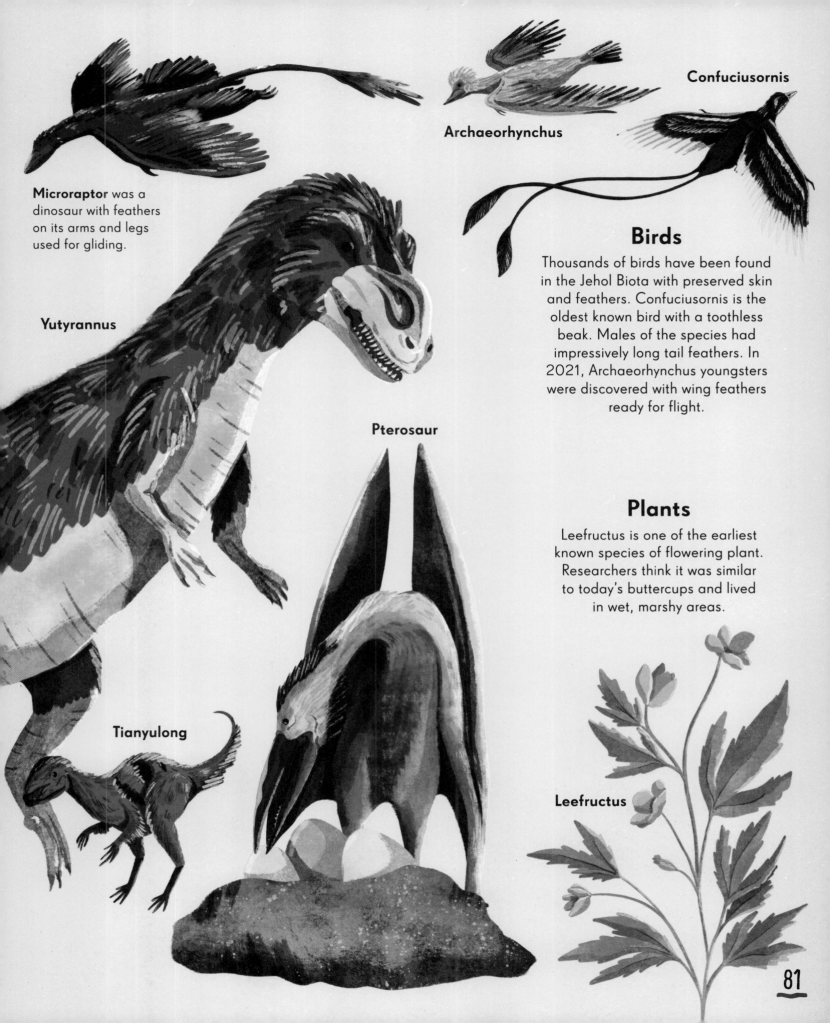

Confuciusornis

Archaeorhynchus

Microraptor was a dinosaur with feathers on its arms and legs used for gliding.

Yutyrannus

Pterosaur

Birds

Thousands of birds have been found in the Jehol Biota with preserved skin and feathers. Confuciusornis is the oldest known bird with a toothless beak. Males of the species had impressively long tail feathers. In 2021, Archaeorhynchus youngsters were discovered with wing feathers ready for flight.

Plants

Leefructus is one of the earliest known species of flowering plant. Researchers think it was similar to today's buttercups and lived in wet, marshy areas.

Tianyulong

Leefructus

THE COLORFUL PSITTACOSAURUS

In 1923 paleontologists announced a dinosaur called Psittacosaurus. It was a type of ceratopsian, with horns on the side of its face and a **parrotlike beak** that it used to eat plants. Unlike its relative Triceratops it was small, measuring only about 5 ft (1.5 m) long. Since its discovery, more than 400 individuals have been found across Asia— ranging from China to Mongolia and Siberia. But one specimen from the Jehol Biota of China was particularly special.

Not only was it almost complete, it also had an extraordinary amount of soft tissue preserved. Soft tissue means the parts of an animal that don't usually survive the fossilization process. The paleontologists were delighted and stunned to find **skin, scales, and even color pigment!** As a result, they were able to create an extremely complete reconstruction of what this Psittacosaurus looked like.

From the bones, the scientists could tell that the individual was between six and seven years old, so not yet fully grown. It had around 100 spectacular bristles toward the end of its tail.

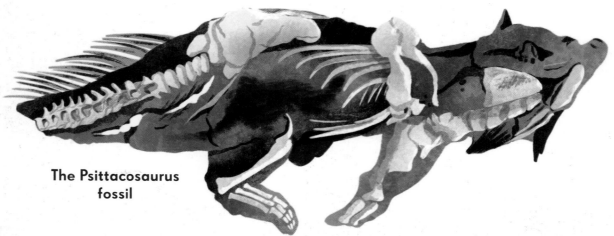

The Psittacosaurus fossil

Psittacosaurus also had large eyes, so it probably lived in a low-light environment, perhaps under a forest canopy. It had three different kinds of scales: large flat scales, smaller angular scales, and round pebble-like scales. Black and amber-brown were the dominant colors, and the pattern of the colors showed Psittacosaurus used **countershading**. This is a type of camouflage usually used by prey animals, where they're darker on the back and lighter on the belly (like a penguin). This would have helped it hide from predators such as Dilong as it snuck through the forest.

THE WONDERS OF LAS HOYAS

The Las Hoyas Lagerstätte in Spain is famous for its well-preserved early Cretaceous life, dating from around 128 million years ago. Back then it was a vast **subtropical wetland** with a seasonal climate. During periods of drought, layers of bacteria flourished in the shallow water, forming smelly mats. These mats may have formed a seal around the remains of animals, helping preserve even the most delicate structures—like fish eyeballs!

One of the unusual dinosaurs that roamed these wetlands was **Pelecanimimus**, a type of ornithomimosaur (an ostrich dinosaur). As its name suggests, it had a skin pouch under its lower jaw, kind of like a pelican.

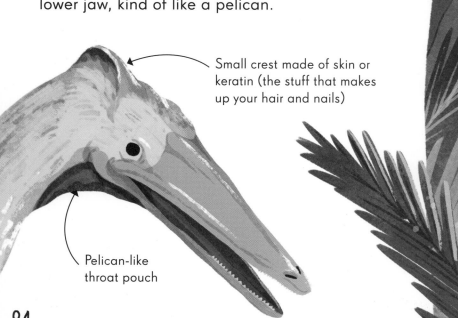

Small crest made of skin or keratin (the stuff that makes up your hair and nails)

Pelican-like throat pouch

Pelecanimimus also had a soft crest on the back of its head, and fossils suggest it might have had feathers. Most ornithomimosaurs don't have teeth, but Pelecanimimus had around 220! And the teeth stopped about a third of the way back on the top jaw, making a long, flat area that might have been used for ripping up small prey.

Now, Pelecanimimus wasn't the only unique dinosaur from Las Hoyas. The nearly complete skeleton of Concavenator—a 20 ft (6 m) long, shark-toothed predator with feathers on its forearms—was found in 2003. It took paleontologists seven years to prepare the specimen. When they were finished, they discovered that there were elongated spines on some of the back bones just before its hips. Concavenator had a **humpback!** To this day the scientists are unsure what the hump was for. Some have suggested it stored fat, like a camel's hump, while others think it was used for display. You never know, maybe Concavenators impressed each other with their spectacular back humps!

THE BLOCK OF RAPTORS

Utahraptor was announced to the world in 1993. It is the largest dromaeosaur (or raptor to you and me) ever found, but it was only known from a few bones and a **giant sickle-shaped claw**. Then, in 2001, college student Matthew Stikes was doing research north of Arches National Park in Utah when he made a grisly discovery. He stumbled across what looked like a human arm bone! He quickly reported his discovery, and it turned out he had found part of a dinosaur foot. Paleontologists headed to the site in 2005. This time they discovered several skeletons.

However, it didn't prove to be an easy excavation. The block that contained the bones weighed several tons and was located way up near the top of a ridge. It took almost **ten years** to get the megablock ready to move. Finally, in 2014, it was slowly dragged off the ridge with an excavator and loaded onto a truck that took it to a museum.

Already over 3,500 hours have been spent preparing this megablock—and there's still more to be done! So far the paleontologists have found two plant-eating iguanodont dinosaurs and multiple Utahraptors, including one large adult, ten juveniles, and three that are probably less than a year old. These babies are tiny—the front part of their snouts is only about the size of a penny!

So, what happened? Well, this megablock formed from dangerous **quicksand**. The iguanodonts may have become stuck first. Their calls, or the smell of their carcasses, attracted the Utahraptors, probably thinking they were going to get an easy meal. But they rapidly became stuck in the quicksand when their feathers were weighed down with mud. What paleontologists don't know is whether the Utahraptors were part of a family group or if they got stuck separately. Maybe the megablock will reveal more secrets in the future...

SHAPE-SHIFTING
DINOSAURS

The first dinosaur reconstructions are from the 1850s, and our understanding of them has changed a lot since! Dinosaurs have gone from slow-moving, tail-dragging lizards to agile creatures with complex lives.

DINOSAUR SCIENCE IS CONSTANTLY EVOLVING.

1850s

1850s

1960s

Megalosaurus

The first dinosaur to be scientifically named, in 1824. Originally it was thought it walked on four legs and was 39 ft (12 m) long. Today we think it walked on two legs and was 20–30 ft (6–9 m) long.

Iguanodon

First thought to be a giant iguana with a spike on its nose! Paleontologists now know the spikes were on its "thumbs" and were probably used to defend itself against predators.

Deinonychus

This discovery made scientists think dinosaurs were warm-blooded, due to their body shape. We still think this is true, but we also now believe Deinonychus was covered in feathers!

Today

Hylaeosaurus

The first depictions showed a single row of spikes down the back. Palaeontologists now understand that this armored dinosaur had spikes lined in two rows along its sides.

Diplodocus

Scientists thought Diplodocus had a sprawling posture and was so heavy it spent most of its time in the water. Today we think it walked with its legs under its body and lived on land.

Stegosaurus

The classic idea of Stegosaurus gave off major Godzilla vibes by walking on two legs with spikes on its back and plates on its tail. This is the opposite of what we know today!

THE SEAFARING ANKYLOSAUR

In 2011, a man named Shawn Funk was operating a digger the size of a house when he noticed some interesting patterns on the rocks that were falling down in front of him. Paleontologists confirmed they were dinosaur bones and worked to excavate the fossils. But something was not quite right. These rocks had been formed **under a sea**. How on Earth did a dinosaur get there?

The unusual specimen took six years to prepare. It was a new type of ankylosaur called **Borealopelta** and it was built like a tank. To the delight of the scientists it was also nearly complete—and preserved in 3D! And despite 110 million years passing, 186 of its impressive armored plates, called osteoderms, were still in place on its back.

Remarkably, the fossil had also preserved soft tissues like tendons, scales, and skin impressions. Thanks to this, paleontologists could tell this fortress of a dinosaur was reddish brown and lighter on its belly. Like Psittacosaurus (see pages 82–83) it possibly used countershading as camouflage to hide from predators—though you'd need a lot of luck to conceal a tank!

Borealopelta was found in an area that was once the Western Interior Seaway, a shallow inland sea that split North America in two. So, how did this heavy landlubber dinosaur get buried 250 miles (400 km) offshore? Well, paleontologists think it died near a river, where its carcass became bloated. Then it must have floated out to sea in a process called **"bloat-and-float."** As the body started breaking down, it sank to the bottom of the sea. Due to the weight of its armor, it landed upside-down in the soft mud, perfectly preserving it for us to find millions of years later.

Borealopelta was found here!

THE GIANT OF GIANTS

Every paleontologist gets asked, "What is the biggest dinosaur?" And it's actually a really hard question to answer! A lot of the time they only have a few isolated bones of a dinosaur, and the best they can do is make estimates. However, one of the contenders for the crown of the largest dinosaur is a giant called **Patagotitan**.

As we've already established in this book, Argentina is a great place to find dinosaurs. Everything we know about Patagotitan is based on six partial skeletons found in the same 101-million-year-old quarry in the Argentinian desert. And research on the bones suggested the animals the scientists found hadn't finished growing... Adults were estimated to weigh almost 77 tons and were **longer than a blue whale**. However, recently there has been some debate about how big this dinosaur really was. In 2020, researchers slimmed down Patagotitan to a measly 63 tons.

PATAGOTITAN'S HEART WAS THE SIZE OF AN ADULT HUMAN.

Regardless, Patagotitan was an enormous animal that needed to eat an equally large amount of food. Unfortunately, paleontologists did not find a skull at the quarry, but they did find a single, small, **peg-like tooth**. This may not sound like much, but it revealed lots of secrets. This plant-eater used its teeth to nip off plants and swallow them whole—it didn't chew. It ate tough, fibrous plants like ferns and conifers. Since these plants are low in nutrition, Patagotitan had to eat an estimated 1,430 lbs (650 kg) of food every day. That's about five times the amount an African elephant eats!

While adult Patagotitans didn't have to worry about predators, youngsters probably did. Paleontologists found 80 teeth from Tyrannotitan in the same quarry. Tyrannotitan was a member of the shark-tooth dinosaur group known as Carcharodontosaurids. This **apex predator** was almost as large as a T. rex, and a baby Patagotitan would have made a delicious dinner for it.

There's still lots we don't know about Patagotitan. If only we could find a skull...

THE GEMSTONE DINOSAURS

Lightning Ridge is a small town in the outback of New South Wales, Australia. Despite being so remote, it is world famous for the **gemstone opals** that are found there. In the 1980s a miner named Bob Foster was 32 ft (10 m) underground digging for the precious gemstones. To find opals he would break open rocks, looking for telltale flashes of iridescent blue.

Some of the opals were oddly shaped, kind of resembling **horse hooves**. Bob was puzzled. He started setting them aside until he had about two suitcases full. Then he took them to the Australian Museum in Sydney—almost 500 miles (800 km) away—to see what the experts made of them.

The museum paleontologists were shocked—Bob had found dinosaur bones that had fossilized into opal! They quickly organized an excavation of the mine and found around 100 dinosaur bones, 60 of which were from a large adult. The other bones were from juveniles. All in all, they found remains of at least four individuals that may have been part of a herd. In honor of Bob, the **Iguanodon-like dinosaurs** were named Fostoria.

Fostoria lived about 100 million years ago when this part of Australia was a vast floodplain. Lakes, lagoons, and rivers flowed into the Eromanga Inland Sea, a seaway that covered most of eastern Australia during the Cretaceous. The dinosaurs that lived here probably didn't expect they'd one day turn into colorful gemstones!

Dinosaur bone turned into chunks of opal over millions of years.

CREATURES OF THE
SHALLOW SEA

During the Cretaceous the climate was warmer than it is today. Sea levels were also higher and ocean water flowed onto North America. By 100 million years ago the continent was split in two by the Western Interior Seaway, home to lots of amazing creatures. The rise of the Rocky Mountains eventually drained the seaway, and by 70 million years ago it was basically gone.

Platyceramus was a giant clam that made massive pearls!

Western Interior Seaway

Laramidia

Archelon is the largest known turtle in history. It was the size of a car!

Hesperornis was a flightless bird with teeth. It had tiny wings and swam using powerful hind legs.

Meet the neighbors

The Western Interior Seaway was shallow, only 2,600 ft (800 m) deep. For comparison, the average depth of the Mediterranean Sea is 5,000 ft (1,500 m). The warm sunlit waters of the seaway supported thriving ecosystems that were dominated by giant swimming reptiles.

Tylosaurus was a type of predatory marine reptile known as a mosasaur.

Uintacrinus had ten long arms. It lived in free-floating colonies.

Nyctosaurus was a pterosaur with a large forked crest on its head.

Parapuzosia was a large ammonite that preyed on turtles, fish, sharks, and even small mosasaurs.

A different world

Scientists call the "island continents" formed by the seaway Appalachia and Laramidia.

Appalachia

Xiphactinus was a predatory fish with a big appetite!

Elasmosaurus had a neck up to 20 ft (6 m) long. It was slow-moving and ate small fish.

Aquilolamna had extremely long, winglike fins that were used to glide through the water.

SEARCHING FOR SPINOSAURUS

Paleontologists have known about Spinosaurus for over 100 years. However, they only had bits and pieces of bone to work with, which meant they knew very little about this **mysterious dinosaur** that lived 97 million years ago. Over time, as more exciting discoveries have been made, our understanding of Spinosaurus has changed.

The story begins in 1912, when a fossil collector found a partial skeleton of a large theropod (a dinosaur belonging to the same family as T. rex) in western Egypt. Three years later the German paleontologist Ernst Freiherr Stromer von Reichenbach named it Spinosaurus. It had a long, narrow snout and teeth shaped like cones, which was unusual for a theropod. It also had **large spines** lining its back, meaning it had a sail! The first reconstruction showed Spinosaurus in a kangaroo-like posture, with a head similar to Allosaurus.

Some time later, the bones were put on display in a museum in Munich, Germany. This would be the last place anyone would ever see them. During World War II, Ernst begged the head of the museum to move the specimens somewhere safer, but tragically it never happened. On April 24, 1944, the Spinosaurus bones were destroyed by a British Royal Air Force **bombing raid** on Munich. Only notes, drawings, and two photographs of the original specimen survived.

After that, a few fragments of Spinosaurus were found across North Africa, but none of these finds told us anything new about this dinosaur. Then in 2005 researchers announced new specimens from Morocco. The fossils told the paleontologists that Spinosaurus was 52–59 ft (16–18 m) long, possibly the largest theropod dinosaur that ever existed! But how exactly did it live? To answer that, the paleontologists needed more bones...

Nizar Ibrahim was in the Sahara desert of Morocco in 2008, looking for dinosaur bones. While passing through a village, a **mustached local fossil collector** stopped Nizar and showed him a box full of fossils. One specimen in particular caught his attention. It was a long, flat, bladelike bone.

Nizar and a team of paleontologists returned to try to find the mustached man in 2013. It took them weeks, but they finally located him and he guided them to the site where he'd found the fossils. There, the team found more Spinosaurus bones, revealing that the dinosaur had short, powerful legs and dense bones. It had the features of an animal that liked to swim!

Now there was just one missing piece of the puzzle: the tail. The search continued for more Spinosaurus bones in 2018 and 2019. Nizar's team worked in scorching temperatures to remove tons of sandstone. But eventually they were successful, finding a nearly complete tail. And to their surprise it was **shaped like a paddle!** They used a robotic model that calculated that the Spinosaurus tail was eight times more powerful in water than a normal theropod tail. This supported their idea that Spinosaurus was an aquatic predator.

In 2021, another team of scientists had a different idea. While they agreed that Spinosaurus was a swimmer, they didn't believe it would have been agile enough to catch quick aquatic prey. Instead they thought it was probably more like a heron, snapping up fish from the shallows. Either way, Spinosaurus is the most aquatic dinosaur found so far!

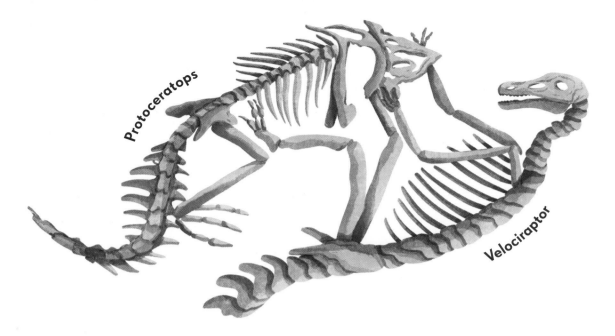

Protoceratops

Velociraptor

FIGHT TO THE DEATH

Seventy-five million years ago the Gobi Desert of Mongolia was pretty similar to today—dominated by sand dunes and the occasional green oasis. Protoceratops, a small horned dinosaur, was heading home after a long day of grazing on plants. As the sun disappeared, twilight fell across the desert. In the darkness, a **Velociraptor** blinked open its large eyes. It was just starting its day. The events that brought these two dinosaurs together are unknown, but they would soon come face-to-face.

During an expedition to the Gobi Desert in 1971, a team led by Polish paleontologist Dr. Zofia Kielan-Jaworowska made an incredible discovery. The team noticed white bone fragments in a yellow sandstone, which turned out to be part of the Protoceratops. As the excavation continued, they found something very unexpected: a complete Velociraptor. And the two seemed to be locked in combat! They were nicknamed "The Fighting Dinosaurs."

The Velociraptor was holding the face of the Protoceratops with its left hand and digging its **sickle-shaped toe claw** into its throat. But the Velociraptor had its right leg trapped under its opponent's body—and its right arm wedged in the jaws of Protoceratops! This was a fight to the death, and unfortunately there was no winner. Shortly after they died locked together, the two dinosaurs were buried in sand, probably from a sandstorm. Their fight was immortalized forever!

EGG MOUNTAIN

About 78 million years ago in what's now Montana, a wide floodplain was bustling with activity. It was nesting season for a group of duck-billed dinosaurs known as **Maiasaura**. Each shallow, bowl-shaped nest held up to 20 eggs. The nests were spaced around 23 ft (7 m) apart—about the length of an adult Maiasaura. And then disaster struck: A nearby river burst its banks and buried some of the nests.

In 1978, Marion Brandvold, owner of the local Rock Shop in Bynum, spotted some small, gray fossils on a hill. She recognized that they were bones and collected them. Later that year, paleontologist Jack Horner and schoolteacher Bob Makela stopped by the Rock Shop. Marion showed them her **coffee can full of tiny bones**. They immediately identified them as baby duck-billed dinosaurs.

The two returned the following year with a field crew and started digging. They found bones from 15 baby Maiasaura at Marion's site, meaning these were the first known dinosaur nests to contain hatchlings! Nearby, a volunteer discovered large pieces of eggshell on top of a hill. This was the first dinosaur egg found in North America. The site was called **Egg Mountain**.

The paleontologists uncovered a wealth of information about Maiasaura. Just like human babies, freshly hatched Maiasaura couldn't walk. This was because their bones weren't fully formed. Despite this, their teeth showed signs of wear, so scientists think that at least one parent brought back food to the nest. This was the first evidence that dinosaurs took care of their young!

Researchers also looked at the inside of the bones, to figure out how a Maiasaura grew from a baby to an adult. They discovered that it happened incredibly fast. Within a year these 18-in (45-cm) hatchlings would grow to be a whopping 10 ft (3 m) long! And they didn't stop there—they would continue growing until they reached full size at the age of eight.

MUSICAL MONSTERS

In a coastal swamp 76 million years ago, the sun was just starting to rise. A dense fog blanketed the edges of the surrounding forest. Suddenly a twig snapped. Something was nearby... A loud, low sound broke through the morning calm. Then another... and another. Soon several tuba-like bellows were joining together! From the mist, huge shadowy figures began to emerge. A **herd of Parasaurolophus** were greeting the new day with a dawn chorus, just like birds do.

The first Parasaurolophus fossils were found in 1920, but the specimen was only half complete. It had everything from the skull to the hips, but it was missing most of the hind legs and tail. Only a few other fragments have been found since the first partial skeleton.

Now... what's with that long head crest? There have been a lot of ideas about the purpose of this structure. Could it have been a snorkel or used for smelling?

These ideas were abandoned in favor of a theory that the head crests were used to make noises. In 1981, American paleontologist David Weishampel tested this idea. He was able to mathematically show that the crest could produce low-frequency noises that could travel over long distances. Then he did what all good scientists do—he made **a model of the crest** using a plastic pipe! And it kind of sounded like a tuba when he blew through it. Other research backed up the theory by showing that Parasaurolophus could hear the range of sounds made by the crest. Many scientists also think these impressive crests would have been used as a form of display.

Later, in 2009, a school student found the most complete skeleton of a new Parasaurolophus species—but this one was a youngster. The baby was nicknamed "Joe" and was 8 ft (2.5 m) long. And despite being only a quarter of the size of an adult, Joe was already starting to grow its crest!

Joe's crest

MEET THE
FRILLY DINOSAURS

The ceratopsians appeared in the Jurassic, around 170 million years ago. They started out small, walked on two legs, and had very small frills. During the Cretaceous they became much larger. They walked on four legs and had horns and elaborate bony neck frills. Paleontologists think these frills were used for defense or for fighting, but also as an impressive form of display.

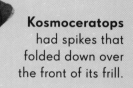

Kosmoceratops had spikes that folded down over the front of its frill.

Einiosaurus had a flattened nasal horn that curved forward. It reached adult size in five years but never stopped slowly growing!

Sinoceratops was discovered in China. It had a large skull with at least ten curved clawlike spikes on the back of its frill.

A **Diabloceratops** skull was removed from a remote field site using a helicopter.

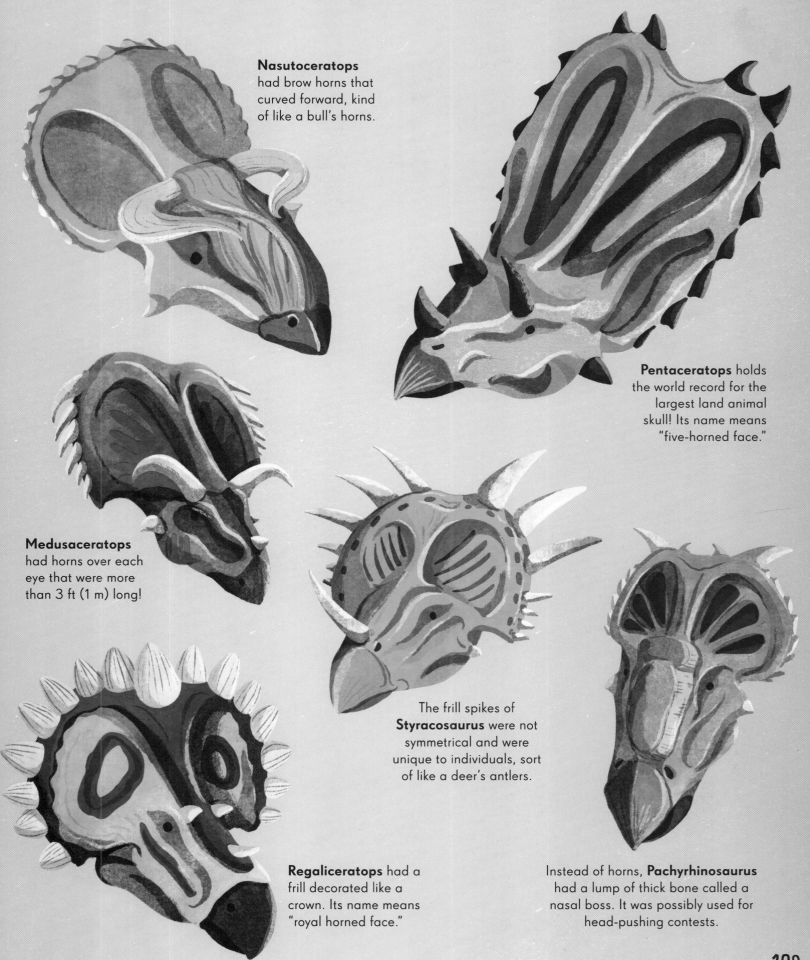

Nasutoceratops had brow horns that curved forward, kind of like a bull's horns.

Pentaceratops holds the world record for the largest land animal skull! Its name means "five-horned face."

Medusaceratops had horns over each eye that were more than 3 ft (1 m) long!

The frill spikes of **Styracosaurus** were not symmetrical and were unique to individuals, sort of like a deer's antlers.

Regaliceratops had a frill decorated like a crown. Its name means "royal horned face."

Instead of horns, **Pachyrhinosaurus** had a lump of thick bone called a nasal boss. It was possibly used for head-pushing contests.

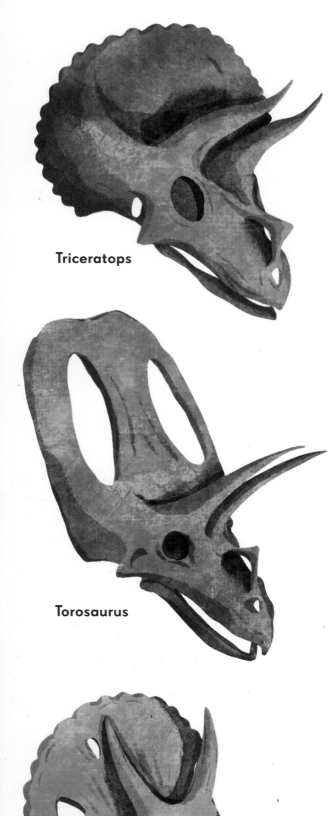

Triceratops

Torosaurus

Nedoceratops

TRICERATOPS VS. TOROSAURUS

Triceratops is the most famous ceratopsian of all time. Another ceratopsian, Torosaurus, looked pretty similar and was believed to be closely related. Dinosaur science, however, is always changing. Over the course of a ten-year study called the **Hell Creek Project**, researchers formed a new theory about the two dinosaurs.

During the project, almost half of the fossils collected were from Triceratops, including 30 skulls from dinosaurs of different ages. The team found it much harder to find Torosaurus fossils, and when they did, the skulls were all large. The paleontologists John Scannella and Jack Horner looked at thin slices of bone under a microscope. It appeared Torosaurus had more developed bone than Triceratops, meaning it was older...

Triceratops and Torosaurus had been considered two different species, but John and Jack argued that Torosaurus was actually an **adult version** of Triceratops! And since Triceratops had been named first, Torosaurus would no longer be valid (poor Torosaurus). Not everyone agreed though, and to make matters worse there was another species to consider—Nedoceratops.

This ceratopsian had holes in its frill like Torosaurus, and John and Jack figured it was also a Triceratops at a different stage of its life. Meanwhile, other scientists discovered that Triceratops and Torosaurus were not always found at the same places, and that the holes in Nedoceratops's frill were formed by **injury or illness**. Most importantly, they looked at how the bones were fused together, which is a general indicator of age. They found that some Torosaurus had areas that were not fused—so they weren't adults! And some of the smaller Triceratops turned out to be older than expected. So is the debate over? Far from it! Paleontologists will continue to discuss these ceratopsians until fossil evidence is found that settles the argument.

MYSTERY OF THE STOLEN FOSSILS

On a rainy day in the Gobi Desert, Mongolia, in 1965, Polish paleontologist Zofia Kielan-Jaworowska was looking around her dig site because it was too wet to excavate. While searching, she discovered some large bones poking out of a 70-million-year-old sandstone. They turned out to be an enormous set of arms tipped with huge claws! The dinosaur was named **Deinocheirus**, and it was believed to be a giant meat-eating theropod.

For a long time, nothing else was found of Deinocheirus, so in 2008 scientists decided to head to the original site. Using just two **black-and-white photos** from 1965, they matched up the rocks to find the exact spot where Deinocheirus had been dug up. And it was a success! They unearthed more Deinocheirus bone fragments, some of which even had bite marks from the carnivore Tarbosaurus.

The following year the team discovered a more complete skeleton. Sadly, illegal fossil poachers had found it first! They had taken the showy parts, like the skull, claws, and feet, but left the rest of the skeleton. This specimen showed that Deinocheirus was a gigantic **ornithomimosaur** (ostrich-like dinosaur). The team also learned that a poached specimen they had found in 2006 was a young Deinocheirus. Between the three specimens they almost had a complete skeleton—they were just missing the skull and feet.

Then, in 2011, Belgian paleontologist Pascal Godefroit was contacted by a fossil dealer in France. The dealer wanted Pascal to see a **weird specimen** he'd been asked to prepare by a private collector. Pascal realized this was something new and contacted the expert Phil Currie, who quickly jumped on a plane to Belgium. He was stunned by the fossils—not only were they from Deinocheirus, they were from the 2009 poached specimen!

Finally, paleontologists had the whole skeleton, and it was really bizarre. Deinocheirus was **duck-billed** and humpbacked. It reached lengths over 33 ft (10 m). It also had a bone at the end of its tail for feather attachments. Fish scales were found with the fossils, indicating that this dinosaur ate both meat and plants and lived in freshwater habitats. It would have been quite a sight to see!

CLASH OF THE BONEHEADS

WHACK! Two large Pachycephalosaurus slowly backed away to size each other up. They pawed at the ground with their feet, sending dirt flying behind them. Then once again they lunged toward each other with heads lowered—**WHACK!** They slammed their thick, domed heads together. At least that's what paleontologists have always thought these boneheads did. But was it actually possible?

For decades, researchers have been trying to figure this out. A study from 2004 looked at the structure of seven Pachycephalosaurus skull bones. It found that the spongy-looking bone in the domes was young and still growing. This meant it was probably not from adults that liked to engage in headbutting. The domes, the scientists thought, were more likely to be used for **impressive visual display** and not combat.

But in 2008, scientists used computers to simulate headbutting collisions between the dinosaurs. They found that Pachycephalosaurus could handle very high-energy impacts because its thick skull **protected the brain**. And if the skull was covered in keratin, like a rhino's horn, it would have softened the blow. Then a new skull dome was discovered that was covered in dents caused by infected injuries. Later, the team discovered that 22% of Pachycephalosaurus skulls show similar signs of trauma. The injuries also occurred at the top of the skull, where most impacts would happen. So maybe these boneheads did like to clash heads after all!

Maybe the males headbutted during mating season, like deer.

THE GIANT PTEROSAURS

After flying over 9,000 miles (14,000 km), a pair of pterosaurs the size of small planes landed in what's now Jordan in the Middle East. When standing they were **as tall as giraffes**—much larger than the local predatory dinosaurs, the abelisaurs. These giant pterosaurs were like storks and would walk or wade, catching whatever was unlucky enough to cross their path.

Arambourgiania was part of a group of enormous pterosaurs called the azhdarchids that ruled during the late Cretaceous. The most famous member is Quetzalcoatlus, but Arambourgiania was even larger, and was actually the first azhdarchid discovered.

All azhdarchids are known from only a few pieces of bone, and pterosaur bone is notoriously bad at fossilizing. The first fossil was found in the early 1940s. The bone was broken, but it was still 24 in (62 cm) long! The French paleontologist Camille Arambourg thought it was a wing bone, but by the 1970s paleontologists realized it was actually a giant neck bone—making Arambourgiania the largest flying creature of all time!

This azhdarchid was originally named **Titanopteryx**, which is a really cool name. However, in 1987 it was changed to Arambourgiania (after our friend Camille) because the name "Titanopteryx" was already in use. *By what*, you may be wondering? Say hello to the original Titanopteryx—a fly named in 1934!

ARAMBOURGIANIA'S NECK WAS 10 FT (3 M) LONG!

KING OF THE
TYRANT LIZARDS

Tyrannosaurus rex is the most famous dinosaur of all time. Its name means "King of the Tyrant Lizards," and it's no wonder that this predator has captured the public's imagination. About 50 partial skeletons have been found so far. An adult T. rex had around 60 banana-sized serrated teeth and needed to eat a huge amount of meat every day by hunting or scavenging.

SUE

SUE is the most complete T. rex ever found— about 90% of the skeleton has been dug up. Using growth rings in the bones, paleontologists discovered that SUE reached full size at the age of 19 and died when it was 28 years old. SUE was also infected with a parasite that caused sores on its mouth.

T. rex may have had feathers.

The human Sue

SUE the T. rex is named after its discoverer, Susan Hendrickson. On August 12, 1990, the amateur fossil hunter was exploring an area of South Dakota when she noticed dinosaur bones sticking out of a cliff. It took the crew 17 days to excavate the skeleton.

Scales and feathers

Since relatives of T. rex had feathers, some scientists think T. rex was feathered at some point in its life. However, T. rex skin impressions from the neck, pelvis, and tail show no feather filaments, just scales. But not all of the skin was preserved, so it's still possible!

Mother rex

In 2005, Mary Schweitzer and her team announced that they had found in a T. rex a type of bone previously only known from egg-laying female birds. This meant that this T. rex was a female that died during egg-laying season.

King of the poops

The world's largest carnivore coprolite (fossilized poop) might be from a T. rex and has been nicknamed "Barnum." It's filled with crushed bone.

T. REX GROWS UP

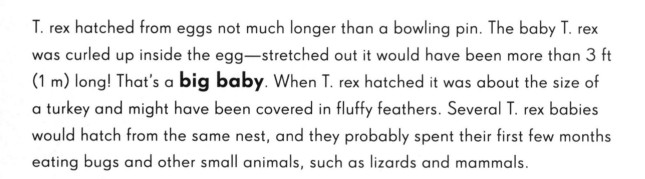

T. rex is known as one of the largest and fiercest predators to ever walk the Earth, but what most people don't know is that T. rex babies were probably pretty cute! This carnivore started out small just like any other dinosaur. No eggs or babies of T. rex have been found yet, but paleontologists can use closely related species to piece together the life story of this incredible dinosaur.

T. rex hatched from eggs not much longer than a bowling pin. The baby T. rex was curled up inside the egg—stretched out it would have been more than 3 ft (1 m) long! That's a **big baby**. When T. rex hatched it was about the size of a turkey and might have been covered in fluffy feathers. Several T. rex babies would hatch from the same nest, and they probably spent their first few months eating bugs and other small animals, such as lizards and mammals.

The youngest T. rex fossils we've found were from a one-year-old nicknamed **"Chomper."** This youngster was a skinny and agile hunter, capable of speeding through the undergrowth to avoid anything that might want to eat it. Throughout its youth, T. rex kept growing. By the age of 13, it was over 20 ft (6 m) long but had a weaker bite than a crocodile. Then, between the ages of 14 and 18, it started to grow rapidly. By the age of 15, this teenager's long, thin skull had turned into the classic T. rex shape. Prey beware!

Chomper

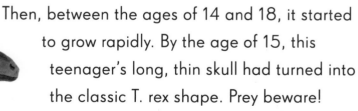

At T. rex's 18th birthday it weighed over 6,600 lb (3,000 kg) and could start **having babies of its own**. Fully grown, T. rex probably didn't have any natural predators, since it was now over 39 ft (12 m) long and had the strongest bite of any land animal. Over the next ten years T. rex's growth would slow, stopping two to three years before it died—usually around the age of 30. The other dinosaurs of the time wouldn't have been sad to see it go!

THE CRATER OF DOOM

For a long time scientists didn't know what happened to the dinosaurs, just that 66 million years ago they went extinct (well... except for birds). How did this happen? In the mid-1970s Walter Alvarez was doing research in Italy when he found a thin layer of clay in some rocks. It possibly marked the boundary between the Cretaceous (when the last of the non-avian dinosaurs lived) and the Paleocene (the period after that). Walter scratched his head and wondered, *If this band of clay was the right age, did it have anything to do with the death of the dinosaurs?*

To date the clay Walter started working with his father, the physicist Luis Alvarez. Luis suggested they test the clay for the chemical element iridium. There's very little iridium in Earth's crust, but there's lots of it in **meteorites from outer space.** Over thousands of years meteor dust containing iridium slowly rains down to Earth and builds up in the ground. Luis figured that if the clay band had formed quickly, there wouldn't have been time for iridium to accumulate. However, their samples had up to 120 times more iridium than expected! What could have caused both the high levels of iridium and an extinction?

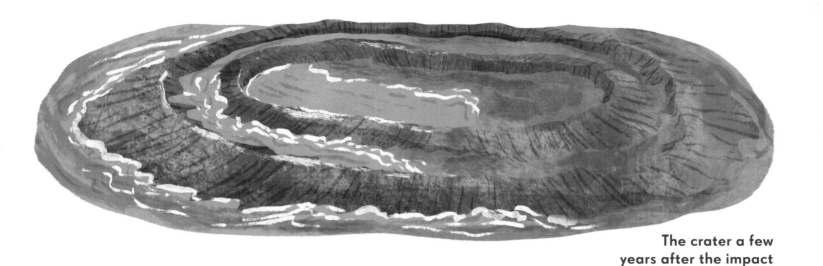

The crater a few years after the impact

They started thinking about the dust thrown into the air by the impact from a giant space rock. If the collision was large enough, there would be plenty of dust to **block out the sun**. And if there's no sun, plants can't survive. If there are no plants, the whole food chain will collapse.

Luis estimated that a meteorite capable of such devastation would create a gigantic crater. So where was this crater hiding? It turned out someone else had already found it! It was located in the Yucatán Peninsula in Mexico, but the original researchers had thought it was a volcano. One reason why the crater was hard to find in the first place is because it's partially buried in the ocean. The center of the impact was near the community of Chicxulub. Walter nicknamed it "The Crater of Doom."

Today, most people accept Walter and Luis's theory, and more evidence has been found to support it. Not everyone agrees though. One of the biggest counter-arguments suggests that **extreme volcanic eruptions** in India could have caused the extinction. They point to evidence of massive lava flows, suggesting these could have affected the world's climate more than a meteorite impact.

CHAPTER FOUR
THE RECENT PAST

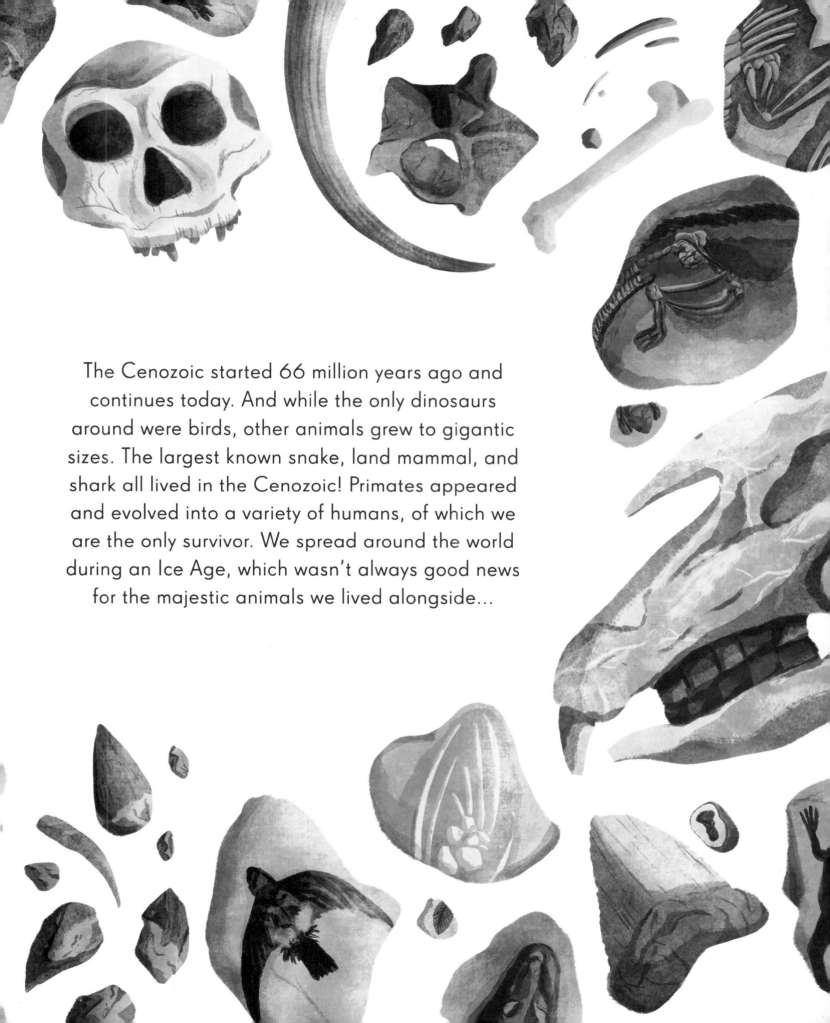

The Cenozoic started 66 million years ago and continues today. And while the only dinosaurs around were birds, other animals grew to gigantic sizes. The largest known snake, land mammal, and shark all lived in the Cenozoic! Primates appeared and evolved into a variety of humans, of which we are the only survivor. We spread around the world during an Ice Age, which wasn't always good news for the majestic animals we lived alongside...

THE AGE OF MAMMALS

So a meteorite hit Earth, obliterating the dinosaurs. What happened next? Trying to study the immediate years after the Cretaceous extinction can be hard because the fossils are very rare. But one site in Colorado was full of surprises. After cracking open a type of rock called a **concretion**, a paleontologist was shocked to find the skull of a mammal! And then the fossils kept coming.

The skull of an ancient mammal inside a concretion

The site recorded the first million years after the
extinction. And *a lot* had happened during that time.
For the first thousand years the landscape was
dominated by ferns and **small mammals** that had
managed to survive the aftermath of the meteorite
impact. Over the next 100,000 years, palms began to
take over and mammals started to grow back to the sizes they
were before the extinction. Then they went on a growth spurt! By
700,000 years post-extinction, much larger mammals like the otter-like
Taeniolabis and wolf-sized, seed-eating Eoconodon scampered across
the Earth. The dinosaurs were gone—the age of mammals had begun!

Eoconodon

Taeniolabis

THE MONSTER SNAKE

Around 58 million years ago, just after the extinction of the dinosaurs, an extremely hot and humid rainforest covered what's now Colombia in South America. It rained a lot, often flooding the forest floor. These were perfect conditions for a **giant predator**. A nearby splash from a crocodile-like animal caught the killer's attention. It quickly swam toward its next meal...

In 2007, Alex Hastings was unpacking fossils that had been collected a few years earlier. They were in a box labelled "crocodile." But Alex was confused. One fossil was clearly not from a crocodile. He showed it to another scientist, Jason Bourque, who recognized it as a **snake back bone**—only it was way bigger than any he'd ever seen. Today the biggest anaconda is over 16 ft (5 m) long. But anaconda back bones looked tiny compared to the fossils!

This kicked off a search for more bones, in both the lab and the field. And there was success—186 back bones and ribs from 28 different snakes were uncovered.

The fossil compared to an anaconda backbone

But how big were these ancient snakes? Scientist P. David Polly created a mathematical model of a snake spine to tell where in the skeleton the fossils went. From this, he could estimate the size of the snake. And whew, was it big! The scientists think it was 43 ft (13 m) long, making it the biggest snake ever discovered. This snake also got a name: **Titanoboa**.

Titanoboa preferred to spend time in the water and was slow on land, like modern anacondas. And this ambush predator had plenty to eat. It lived with huge crocodile-like animals, giant turtles, and jumbo lungfish. Everything but an adult turtle was probably on the menu. Reptiles rely on their surroundings for heat, so the hot jungle climate is probably what allowed this monster snake to reach such enormous sizes.

THE EVIL WINDS

The Messel Pit in Germany records life from about 48 million years ago in stunning detail. Skeletons and soft tissues are preserved, and there are unusually high numbers of animals that don't usually fossilize well, like bats and birds.

What made the fossils at Messel so extraordinary? Well, during the Eocene a dense tropical jungle surrounded Messel Lake. The lake had been created by an **underground volcano** that had erupted, creating a funnel-shaped crater that filled with water. At the bottom of the lake the water was very cold and there was no oxygen to support scavengers. So after an animal died it sank to the bottom undisturbed.

In these cold, still, deep lakes, a gas called carbon dioxide can build up at the bottom. Then earthquakes can cause eruptions of the toxic gas. In Swahili these are called *mazukus*—or "evil winds"—and they can suffocate anything in their path. There's evidence that at Messel Lake this happened lots of times over a million years.

This was bad news for the animals, but great news for paleontologists. At Messel Pit they've found fossils of eight species of bat, many of which still have thin wing membranes. Several of the 70 species of bird found at the site have feather colors and patterns preserved. At least 45 species of mammal have been found, and their fossils are lined with fuzzy hair! Eurohippus was a **tiny ancient horse**; Darwinius is the best-preserved primate in the world and looked a little like a lemur; and Pholidocercus was a hedgehog-like creature with scales on its head. Several hundred species of insect have also been discovered, including jewel beetles, a fly found with flower pollen in its stomach, and a giant ant! The Messel Pit is the gift that keeps on giving.

Eurohippus

Darwinius

Pholidocercus

THE CREATURES OF
TURTLE COVE

The Turtle Cove Assemblage is found in Oregon. Fossils from here are about 30 to 25 million years old and are preserved in a blue-green rock. These fossils record a time of change. The hot subtropical environment of the Eocene was replaced by cooler conditions in the Oligocene. Wooded areas and grasslands covered the landscape in the shadow of volcanoes, and wonderful beasts stalked the land.

Diceratherium was the first rhino to have horns.

Eusmilus was a catlike animal that had a large lower jaw to protect its saber teeth.

Gentilicamelus was a small relative of camels. It was one of the first animals that lived in the newly formed grasslands.

Mesocyon was a dog that grew to the size of a coyote.

Archaeotherium is also called a "hell pig." These cow-sized, piglike animals probably stole kills from other predators.

Ekgmowechashala was a nocturnal (awake at night) primate that ate fruit. Its name means "little cat man" in Sioux.

Miohippus was a small, three-toed ancestor of modern horses.

Stylemys was a tortoise that ate fruit like hackberries and could live to the age of 90.

Merycoidodon was a stocky animal with four-toed hooves and a long tail.

THE GIANT RHINO

In the early 1900s scientists from the United Kingdom and Russia separately found large mammal bones in Asia. However, it wasn't until 1923 that the **gigantic skull** of the same beast was found by a team from the United States. The three countries shared their bones with one another to compare notes. Then they announced to the world one of the largest land mammals that ever lived—Paraceratherium.

Paraceratherium is most closely related to rhinos. It roamed all over Asia from about 34 to 28 million years ago, living in forests. Paraceratherium was a browser that ate the leaves from the very tops of trees. It stood roughly 16 ft (5 m) tall at the shoulder and its neck alone was 8 ft (2.5 m) long. This giant was significantly bigger than modern giraffes and would have made an **awe-inspiring sight** as it lumbered through the woods!

So what happened to this mega beast? Scientists aren't 100% sure, but they think its extinction might have had something to do with another group of large mammals—the gomphotheres. These **elephant-like creatures** were able to push down trees, which caused problems for Paraceratherium, who liked to eat them! New, bigger predators also migrated into Asia and were able to take down large prey, like Paraceratherium calves. Whatever the cause of its extinction, Paraceratherium was gone before the end of the Oligocene.

MEET THE
MEGA SHARK

Swimming through the world's oceans 23 to 3.5 million years ago was a shark. But it wasn't any old shark... Megalodon was the biggest shark that ever lived! For a long time scientists thought Megalodon was related to great white sharks, but now they think that it is an extinct species of mackerel shark. There are many reasons why Megalodon went extinct. The climate cooled and sea levels dropped, and it also faced stiff competition from newly evolved great whites.

Open wide

Megalodon teeth have been known about for a really long time. They were first correctly identified as shark teeth in 1667! The shark's jaws were lined with 276 serrated teeth that were constantly replaced during its life.

The smallest teeth collected show that baby Megalodons were 8.5 ft (2.6 m) long.

The largest Megalodon teeth are around 7 in (18 cm) long!

Jaws

Megalodon is thought to have had a bite force of up to 19 tons. That's the equivalent of having four adult hippos slam down on prey. Oh, and the hippos would be lined with razor-sharp steak knives. Yikes!

Supersized

Sharks are mostly made of cartilage (like your nose and ears), which doesn't fossilize well. This means that we have to estimate Megalodon's size from its teeth. Scientists reckon this giant ranged between 46–79 ft (14–24 m) in length.

Great white shark

Megalodon

Lunch

Many fossil bones have been found with bite marks that match Megalodon teeth. Based on this, researchers think that it mainly ate small- to medium-sized dwarf baleen whales, as well as seals.

Piscobalaena, a dwarf baleen whale

MEGALODON MAY HAVE HAD THE MOST POWERFUL BITE OF ALL TIME.

TREASURES FROM THE DUMP

North of Barcelona lies one of the largest and stinkiest dumps in Spain. In the early 2000s the owners wanted to expand the landfill. Because the surrounding area is known to have fossils, paleontologists had to be on site to make sure nothing important was destroyed. It's a good thing too! Since then, more than **70,000 vertebrate fossils** have been found—including amphibians, reptiles, and birds, as well as more than 75 mammal species.

Pierolapithecus

The most exciting finds are the hominids, or the **great apes**, a group that includes orangutans, gorillas, chimpanzees—and us! The first ape the scientists found was Pierolapithecus, nicknamed "Pau." Pierolapithecus usually moved around on four legs, but it could climb standing straight up, hang from branches, and swing from tree to tree. This was the first step toward walking on two legs, like humans do.

Another hominid, Anoiapithecus, was found in 2004. The male specimen was nicknamed "Lluc." Anoiapithecus had a surprisingly flat face, like ours, instead of one that sticks out, like most other primates. Scientists think this is an example of **convergent evolution**, which is when animals that are not closely related develop similar traits because they live in similar environments. Another example is the similarity between the wings of of pterosaurs and bats.

From the fossils, paleontologists have been able to reconstruct the ancient environment between about 12.5 and 11.5 million years ago. During this period, the environment went from humid, thick forest to dryer, more patchy forest, with grass starting to dominate. It was almost time for the hominids to come down from the trees.

Anoiapithecus

THE WORLD TURNS TO ASH

On a late spring day almost 12 million years ago in what's now Nebraska, a dark cloud appeared on the horizon. For animals living around a nearby watering hole this was not good news. In fact it was very, very bad news. A distant supervolcano had erupted, and soon ash started to fall on the dry savanna. The **ash rained down for several days**, piling up like snow. This was horrible for the animals who breathed it in. Under a microscope, volcanic ash looks like broken glass, and it can cause major lung damage when it's inhaled. The poor animals slowly suffocated to death. The victims included crowned cranes, horned rodents, saber-toothed deer, camels, horses, pot-bellied rhinos, and one giant tortoise.

Other than a little scavenging by bone-crushing dogs, such as Epicyon, the skeletons lay undisturbed until 1971. That year, paleontologist Michael Voorhies spotted white bone in a silvery-gray ash layer. It was the jaw of a baby rhino. The next day he removed the skull, only to find it was connected to neck bones! Mike wasn't ready to excavate a whole skeleton, so he came back later with a small crew. They excavated a large area and found the rest of the baby rhino as well as 11 other complete skeletons, including a **pregnant rhino**. And this was just the beginning. Since then—and continuing to this day—paleontologists, interns, and volunteers have uncovered more than 200 skeletons! Most of them are from Teleoceras, the pot-bellied rhino.

THE WHALE GRAVEYARD

In 2010, during the construction of a highway in Chile's Atacama Desert, workers came across the last thing they expected to find—**whale bones**, and lots of them! Unbelievably, they had uncovered a whale graveyard with dozens of skeletons. Work on the road was scheduled to be completed the next year, so paleontologists from Chile and the United States had to work at a fast pace to try to figure out how the bones had ended up so far inland. Using 3D scanners they quickly mapped the entire site before the fossils were removed from the ground.

The team named this site **Cerro Ballena**, which is Spanish for "whale hill." They excavated 40 individual skeletons, of which 31 were the same species of large baleen whale. They also found two different species of seal, an extinct type of sperm whale, a toothed whale with walrus-like tusks, and—get this—an aquatic sloth!

The scientists pieced together a theory about what had happened. Back in the Miocene, between 9 and 6.5 million years ago, the desert was a muddy area that flooded with the tides every day. All of the whale skeletons were basically complete, preserved belly-up, and they were really close to one another. This suggested that they died out at sea around the same time and were washed onto the mudflat by ocean currents.

So what killed them? The only thing that fits all the evidence is something called a **red tide**. This is when microscopic algae suddenly reproduce on a vast scale, which happens when there's a rapid increase of nutrients in coastal waters. And these blooms can be toxic! Such an event could have killed the animals, setting in motion an epic journey that would end in a desert millions of years later.

THE PEOPLE
IN THE TREES

In 1974, Donald Johanson was working under the hot sun in the Afar region of Ethiopia, East Africa. Suddenly he saw a glimpse of bone. And then another, and another... He followed the trail of bones up the side of a cliff. They turned out to be a partial skeleton—but not just any old skeleton. Donald had found one of our oldest relatives! The skeleton was nicknamed **"Lucy"** and she was 40% complete. Lucy was a species of hominin called Australopithecus who lived about 3.2 million years ago. When Donald found her, she was the oldest and most complete ancient human ancestor ever discovered.

Since her discovery, we've learned a lot about Australopithecus from nearly 400 specimens. On average, they stood between 3 ft (1 m) and 5 ft (1.5 m) tall. From their teeth we can tell that they ate a variety of foods, including fruit, grasses, leaves, insects, small vertebrates, and eggs. Australopithecus had a **small brain**, roughly the size of a grapefruit—that's about a third of the size of a modern human brain (so they weren't as smart as us!).

Most importantly, Lucy's hip and leg bones show that Australopithecus walked on two legs! Since they also had

Lucy's skull

adaptations to climb trees, scientists think that they spent their days walking on the ground, but nested and slept in the safety of the trees.

However, being able to walk upright might have impacted their ability to climb safely. In 2016, researchers scanned Lucy's remains and may have found her cause of death. Lucy had **broken bones** all over her body that suggested she had fallen from a great height, probably from a tree. Today, chimpanzees hang out in trees around 46 ft (14 m) above the ground. A fall from this height would almost certainly be fatal. The researchers found similar fractures on other specimens of Australopithecus, suggesting that falls like this were unfortunately common.

THE DAWN OF
HUMANS

The species Homo sapiens shows up in the fossil record around 300,000 years ago in Africa. Does that name sound familiar to you? That's right—*you* are a Homo sapiens! Our branch of the family tree can be traced back about seven million years to when we split from the other great apes, such as chimpanzees. We're not even the only species of human that has existed. Currently, there are nine other species known, including our most famous cousins, Homo neanderthalensis— the Neanderthals.

Sahelanthropus

Sahelanthropus lived 7–6 million years ago in Africa and was one of our first relatives that could walk on two legs.

Australopithecus

This species goes back 4.2 million years and probably made stone tools, including those found at a site in Kenya. Their hand bones were adapted to use tools. Lucy (see pages 144–145) was an Australopithecus.

Homo habilis

Homo habilis is thought to have scavenged meat and used stone tools. They lived 2.4 million years ago.

Homo erectus

Homo erectus may have been the first humans to use fire and were the first to leave Africa. They were around for 1.8 million years.

Homo floresiensis

These humans lived on the island of Flores in Indonesia from 190,000 to 50,000 years ago. They've been nicknamed "hobbits" because adults were just 3 ft (1 m) tall.

Neanderthals

Neanderthals lived in Europe and Asia from 400,000 to 30,000 years ago. They had advanced tools, wore clothes, made art, took care of each other, and possibly even buried their dead.

Denisovans

A handful of remains of these mysterious humans have been found in Siberia and Tibet. DNA from some of the bones, including a pinkie finger, shows that they lived 400,000 to 30,000 years ago.

THE PIT OF DESPAIR

High up in the Bighorn Mountains of Wyoming, there's a massive hole in the ground. If you are walking or running in a certain direction, it's completely hidden. What you can't see is the opening to a deep, **bell-shaped cave**. And if you accidentally fall in... well, let's just say don't fall in! The drop from the entrance to the cave floor is 92 ft (28 m). The cave formed about 200,000 years ago, and by 150,000 years ago the first of many animals would fall in. The fall was fatal. The deadliest period was between 24,000 and 12,000 years ago, when the cave was located on a path animals frequently traveled along. Today it's known as Natural Trap Cave.

Excavations in the cave started in the 1970s and continued on and off until 2017. And it turned out that this was a cave filled with fossils—over 40,000 specimens have been collected. There are even a bunch of complete skeletons, including several **American cheetahs.** Paleontologists also found specimens of the American lion, at least two species of horse, a giant short-faced bear, woodland musk oxen, and even a camel. In total, around 27 different species have been discovered in the cave, ranging in size from voles to woolly mammoths.

The cave is like a fridge—it stays super cold all year long. This creates the perfect climate for preserving **ancient DNA**, the genetic code found inside all living things that can tell us more about how animals evolved over time.

Scientists looked at the DNA from **dire wolves**, including one from the cave. They found that instead of being closely related to modern gray wolves, dire wolves were an ancient group that formed around 5.7 million years ago. They also discovered that dire wolves evolved in North America, while the ancestors of gray wolves and coyotes came from Europe and Asia, and migrated to North America more recently. Who knows what other secrets the cave will reveal in the future?

GIANTS OF
THE ICE AGE

The most recent Ice Age lasted from about 125,000 to 10,000 years ago. Glaciers covered much of the northern hemisphere. In some places the ice was over 1.9 miles (3 km) thick! Giant mammals called megafauna roamed the world and were followed by humans. During this time, we built our first civilizations and became the last human species still alive.

The **steppe mammoth** was the largest mammoth species and lived in Europe and Asia.

Megaloceros is sometimes called the "Irish elk." It sported the largest antlers in the world.

Megafauna

A combination of cooler climates and bigger habitats allowed so many animals to get so big. However, between 45,000 and 10,000 years ago, 65% of Ice Age megafauna went extinct across the globe. This was probably due to climate change and human hunters.

Glyptodon was an armored, car-sized animal that lived in South America. It is related to modern armadillos.

Thylacoleo was a marsupial lion that lived in Australia. It had large meat-shearing teeth and a powerful bite.

Asia

Beringia

North America

Land bridges

All that ice sucked up a lot of water, which lowered sea levels. This created several land bridges, including one that connected North America and Asia. The exposed land was called Beringia. It allowed some animals, including humans, to travel between the two continents.

Elasmotherium was a Siberian rhino previously thought to have had a massive horn. We now think it was shorter!

Eremotherium was a giant ground sloth the size of a modern elephant. It lived in the Americas.

Smilodon was a saber-toothed cat— not a tiger! It isn't closely related to modern cats.

Diprotodon was the largest marsupial to ever walk the Earth. It lived in Australia.

By 2,000 years ago, **humans** had spread to almost every corner of the globe.

THE LAST MAMMOTHS

The remote Wrangel Island is located off the coast of Russia in the Arctic Sea. This island used to be connected to the mainland, but it was cut off when the ice sheets melted and sea levels rose at the end of the Pleistocene. While most Ice Age megafauna went extinct by 10,000 years ago, one of the most iconic species held on much longer on this remote island—the **woolly mammoth**.

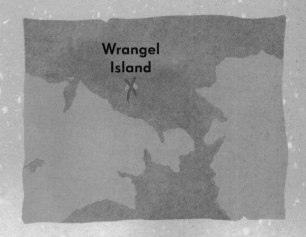

Wrangel Island

The youngest mammoth fossil we've found is a molar tooth from Wrangel Island. Incredibly, this tooth was only 4,300 years old. That means that the mammoth the tooth belonged to was still alive when the **pyramids of Egypt** were being built! Although these mammoths were the ultimate Ice Age survivors, their survival came at a cost. A small population of a few hundred was stranded on the island around 12,000 years ago. And over 6,000 years of isolation, the mammoths interbred with each other. Interbreeding isn't healthy and can cause harmful mutations to develop. As a result, the population started to crash.

The mammoth molar tooth

Scientists were able to extract DNA from the ancient molar and found that it was full of **mutations**. And while it sounds like something from a science fiction movie, scientists were able to resurrect those mutations to see if they were harmful. They found that the Wrangel Island mammoths may not have been able to smell flowers, that their fur was semi-transparent and less thick than normal, and that they had learning difficulties. These mutations probably made the last mammoths more susceptible to extinction. Eventually, after holding out for so long, the mammoths were gone for good.

MAMMOTHS ARE RELATED TO MODERN ELEPHANTS.

GLOSSARY

Arthropod

An invertebrate with jointed legs and a hard outside exoskeleton. Insects, crabs, and spiders are arthropods.

Carnivore

An animal that eats meat.

Concretion

A round, really hard type of rock that forms around an object such as a leaf or bone.

Continent

Any large, unbroken chunk of land, for example Africa today or Pangaea in the past.

Coprolite

Fossilized poop!

DNA

DNA is short for "deoxyribonucleic acid." DNA is found inside living things and contains the genetic instructions for how they will look and behave.

Ecosystem

A community of living things and the environment they live in.

Evolution

How living things gradually change over many generations by surviving and passing down their DNA to their descendants.

Extinction

An event where an entire species dies.

Fossil

Remains and traces of ancient life, usually preserved in rocks.

Geologist

A person who studies the Earth, including rocks and earthquakes.

Herbivore

An animal that eats plants.

Invertebrate

An animal without a backbone, such as a snail.

Mammal

An animal that has hair or fur, is warm-blooded, and has babies that feed on milk from their mothers.

Marsupial

A mammal that keeps its growing babies in a pouch, for example a kangaroo or a koala.

Non-avian dinosaurs

All the dinosaurs that are not birds. They went extinct at the end of the Cretaceous.

Paleontologist

A person who uses fossils to study the history of life.

Predator

An animal that eats other animals.

Prey

An animal that is eaten by other animals.

Primate

A type of mammal from a group that includes lemurs, lorises, tarsiers, monkeys, apes, and humans.

Pterosaur

A flying prehistoric reptile that is not a dinosaur.

Sauropod

A dinosaur that had a small head and a long neck and tail. Some sauropods, such as Patagotitan, grew to enormous sizes.

Soft tissue

Parts of a body that surround organs and bones, for example muscles, cartilage, and skin.

Therapsid

A mammal-like reptile. Therapsids were the dominant land animals about 270 million years ago. They would give rise to true mammals.

Theropod

A dinosaur that had hollow bones and three toes, for example T. rex. Birds evolved from a group of small theropods.

Trilobite

A type of extinct marine arthropod.

Vertebrate

An animal with a backbone, like you!

INDEX

A

Abelisauroids 78, 116
Aetosaurs 47
algae 143
Allosaurus 68–69, 98
Amargasaurus 78–79
Anchiornis 67
ankylosaurs 90–91
Anning, Mary 58–59
Anoiapithecus 139
Antarctica 39, 56–57
apes 139, 146
Aquilolamna 97
Arambourgiania 116
Archaeopteryx 66, 74, 77
Archaeotherium 133
Archean 7
Archelon 96
Argentina 44, 50, 92
armored fish 26–27
armored plates 90
Arthropleura 30
arthropods 20–21, 22, 25, 30–31
Asia 39, 82, 134, 151
Aspidorhynchus 75
Atopodentatus 52
Australia 12, 39, 94–95
Australopithecus 144–145, 146
azhdarchids 116

B

babies 34–35, 87, 105, 120
Beringia 151
"Big Al" (Allosaurus) 68–69
birds 43, 66–67, 81
Borealopelta 90–91
Brodia 31
bugs 30–31
Burgess Shale, Canada 20–21
buzzsaw sharks 32–33

C

Caelestiventus 54–55
Caihong 66
Cambrian 7, 20, 60
camouflage 83, 91
Canada 20, 22, 28
Carboniferous 7, 30
Carcharodontosaurids 93
cartilage 32, 136
Cenozoic 6–7
ceratopsians 82, 108–109,
    110–111
Cerro Ballena, Chile 142–143
Charnia 15
Charnwood Forest, England 14–15
cheetahs 149
Chile 142–143
China 64, 80–81, 82
"Chomper" (T. rex) 120
claws 86, 103, 112

climate change 8, 123
Coelophysis 48–49
Colombia 128
Concavenator 85
concretions 24–25, 126
conifers 77
continents 38–39, 96, 151
convergent evolution 139
Cope, Edward Drinker 70–71
coprolites 48, 59, 76, 119
crests 106–107
Cretaceous 7, 77, 84, 116
    ceratopsians 108
    extinctions 9, 122
    Western Interior Seaway 96
Cryolophosaurus 56–57
Cynodonts 46
Cynognathus 38

D

Darwinius 131
Deinocheirus 112–113
Deinonychus 88
Denisovans 147
Devonian 7, 8, 26–27
Diabloceratops 108
Diceratherium 132
Dickinsonia 17
Dicynodonts 47
Dimorphodon 59
dinosauromorphs 40–41

Diplodocus 50, 89
diseases 68–69
DNA 147, 149, 153
Drepanosaurus 53
dromaeosaurs 86
duck-bills 113

E

Ediacaran Biota 16–17
eggs 43, 104–105, 119, 120
Egypt 98
Einiosaurus 108
Ekgmowechashala 133
Elasmosaurus 97
elephants 135, 153
England 14–15, 58
Eocene 7, 130, 132
Eoconodon 127
Erythrosuchus 52
Ethiopia 144
Eurohippus 131
Eusmilus 132
extinctions 8–9, 122–123, 153

F

feathers 67, 119
ferns 77, 127
fish 26–27, 75
"fishapods" 29

footprints 40–41, 64–65, 76
fossil analysis 24–25, 54–55
fossil collection 58–59, 71
Fostoria 94–95
France 76–77
frills 108–109

G

Gentilicamelus 132
Germany 63, 74, 99, 130
Glossopteris 39
gomphotheres 135

H

Hadean 7
Heleosaurus 34–35
Helicoprion 32–33
Hell Creek Project 110
Herrerasaurus 44–45
Hesperornis 96
Hesperornithoides 67
hip joints 43
Holocene 7
hominids 139, 144, 146–147
horses 133
humans 139, 144, 146–147, 151
humpbacks 85, 113
Hylaeosaurus 89

I

Ice Age 150–151, 152
ichthyosaurs 52, 58, 59
Iguanodons 87, 88, 95
India 39, 123
Ingentia 51
interbreeding 152
Isotelus rex 22

J

jawless fish 27
jaws 32, 136
Jordan 116
Jurassic 7, 50, 68
    ceratopsians 108
    pterosaurs 74–75

K

keratin 78, 84, 115
Kosmoceratops 108
Kulindadromeus 66

L

land bridges 151
Las Hoyas Lagerstätte, Spain
    84–85
Longisquama 53
"Lucy" (hominin) 144–145
Lystrosaurus 38

M

Maiasaura 104–105
mammals 80, 126–127, 134–135
    Ice Age 150–151
    see also humans
mammoths 149, 150, 152–153
Mars 13
Marsh, Othniel Charles 70–71
Mazothairos 30
Medusaceratops 109
megafauna 150–151, 152
Megalodon 136–137
Megalosaurus 88
Meganeura 30
Merycoidodon 133
Mesocyon 132
Mesosaurus 39
Messel Pit, Germany 130–131
meteorites 122–123
Mexico 123
Microraptor 81
Miocene 7, 143
Miohippus 133
Miragaia 72–73
Mongolia 102, 112
Morocco 99–100

N

Nasutoceratops 109
Neanderthals 147
necks 72, 73, 78
Nedoceratops 110–111
nests 104–105, 120, 145
Niger 62
North America 38, 96, 149, 151
Nyctosaurus 97

O

Oligocene 7, 132, 135
opals 94–95
Ordovician 7, 8, 22
ornithomimosaurs 84–85, 112
osteoderms 90
Ostracoderms 27

P

Pachycephalosaurus 114–115
Pachyrhinosaurus 109
Paleocene 7, 122
Paleozoic 6–7
Pangaea 38–39
Paraceratherium 134–135
Parapuzosia 97
Parasaurolophus 106–107
Patagotitan 92–93
Pelecanimimus 84–85

Pentaceratops 109
Permian 7, 8, 30, 32, 39
Perseverance (Mars rover) 13
Pholidocercus 131
Phytosaurs 46
Pierolapithecus 139
Placoderms 8, 26
plants 81
    ferns 77, 127
Platyceramus 96
Plesiosaurus 59
Pleistocene 7, 152
Pliocene 7
Poland 40
poop, fossilized (coprolites) 48,
    59, 76, 119
Portugal 72–73
Precambrian 6–7
primates 131, 133, 139
    see also humans
Prorotodactylus 40–41
Proterozoic 7
Protoceratops 102–103
proto-dinosaurs 40–41
Psittacosaurus 82–83
pterosaurs 54–55, 59, 67, 80
    Arambourgiania 116–117
    Rhamphorhynchus 74–75
Pulmonoscorpius 31

Q

Quetzalcoatlus 116

R

raptors 86–87, 102–103
Rauisuchians 47
red tides 143
Regaliceratops 109
reptiles 42, 46, 54, 80
    snakes 128–129
Rhamphorhynchus 74–75
rhinos 132, 134–135, 140–141
Rhynchosaurs 47
Russia 32, 152

S

Sahelanthropus 146
sauropodomorphs 50
sauropods 50–51, 62, 77
    footprints 64–65
    spiny 78–79
Saurosuchus 44
scales 83, 119
Seirocrinus 60–61
sharks 26, 32–33, 136–137
Sharovipteryx 52
Shonisaurus 52
Shringasaurus 53
Silurian 7
Sinoceratops 108
skulls 108–109, 110, 114–115

Smilodon 151
snakes 128–129
South Africa 34
Spain 63, 84, 138
spines 78, 98
Spinophorosaurus 62–63
Spinosaurus 98–101
stegosaurs 71, 72–73, 89
stromatolites 12, 13
Stylemys 133
Styracosaurus 109
SUE (T. rex) 118–119
synapsids 34–35

T

Taeniolabis 127
tails 101
Tanystropheus 53
Tarbosaurus 112
teeth 43, 93, 136
Temnodontosaurus 58, 59
Temnospondyls 46
tetrapods 28–29
therapsids 35, 46, 47
Titanoboa 128–129
Titanopteryx 116
Torosaurus 110–111
Triceratops 82, 110–111
Triassic 7, 9, 40–41, 46–47, 52–53
Triceratops 82, 110–111
Turtle Cove, US 132–133

Tylosaurus 96
Tyrannosaurus rex (T. rex) 118–119, 120–121
Tyrannotitan 93

U

Uintacrinus 97
United Kingdom 14–15, 58
United States of America 48, 54, 68, 70–71, 86, 104, 126, 132–133, 140, 148
Utahraptors 86–87

V

Velociraptors 102–103
volcanic eruptions 123, 130, 140

W

Western Interior Seaway 91, 96–97
wolves 149
woolly mammoths 149, 150, 152–153

X

Xenoblatta 31
Xiphactinus 97

Y

Yi qi 66
Yutyrannus 80–81

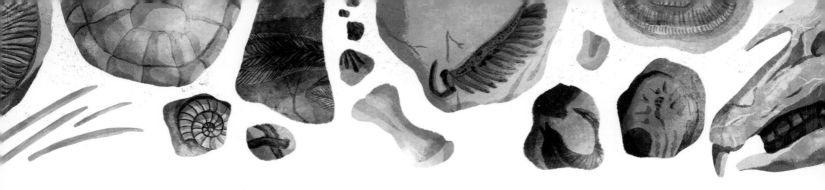

This has been a

NEON SQUID

production

I'd like to thank everyone who encouraged and supported me while I wrote this book, especially my husband, parents, and cat. Also thanks to the multitudes of people who have studied the Earth and shared their discoveries to advance our knowledge.

Author: Kallie Moore
Illustrator: Becky Thorns
Consultant: Amanda Hendrix
US Editor: Allison Singer-Kushnir

Neon Squid would like to thank:

Georgina Coles for proofreading, and Elizabeth Wise for compiling the index.

Created for St. Martin's Press by Neon Squid
The Stables, 4 Crinan Street, London, N1 9XW

EU representative: Macmillan Publishers Ireland Ltd, 1st Floor, The Liffey Trust Centre, 117–126 Sheriff Street Upper, Dublin 1, D01 YC43

10 9 8 7 6 5 4 3 2 1

Printed and bound by Vivar Printing in Malaysia.

ISBN: 978-1-684-49254-1

Published in September 2022.

www.neonsquidbooks.com